BEYOND
THE GREAT DIVIDE

TOURING NORTH AMERICA

SERIES EDITOR
Anthony R. de Souza, *National Geographic Society*

MANAGING EDITOR
Winfield Swanson, *National Geographic Society*

BEYOND THE GREAT DIVIDE

Denver to the Grand Canyon

BY
COTTON MATHER,
P. P. KARAN, and
GEORGE F. THOMPSON

RUTGERS UNIVERSITY PRESS • NEW BRUNSWICK, NEW JERSEY

This book is published in cooperation with the 27th International Geographical Congress, which is the sole sponsor of *Touring North America*. The book has been brought to publication with the generous assistance of a grant from the National Science Foundation/Education and Human Resources, Washington, D.C.

Rutgers University Press
109 Church Street
New Brunswick, New Jersey 08901

The paper used in this book meets the minimum requirements of American National Standard for Information Sciences—Permanence of Paper for Printed Library Materials, ANSI Z39.48-1984.

Library of Congress Cataloging-in-Publication Data

Mather, Cotton, 1918–
    Beyond the Great Divide: Denver to the Grand Canyon / by Cotton Mather, P. P.
Karan, and George F. Thompson. —1st ed.
        p.   cm. —(Touring North America)
    Includes bibliographical references and index.
    ISBN 0-8135-1882-2 (cloth)—ISBN 0-8135-1883-0 (paper)
    1. Colorado—Tours.   2. New Mexico—Tours.   3. Arizona—Tours.
    4. Southwest, New—Tours.   I. Karan, Pradyumna P. (Pradyumna Prasad).
    II. Thompson, George Fletcher.   III. Title.   IV. Series.
F774.3.M38   1992
917.8—dc20   92-10534
                                                                                         CIP

First Edition

Frontispiece: Two beautiful ceramic jugs made in the traditional way, the top one from Acoma Pueblo and the bottom one from Zia Pueblo. Photograph by Cotton Mather.

Series design by John Romer

Typeset by Peter Strupp/Princeton Editorial Associates

△ Contents

PART THREE

RESOURCES

△ Foreword

Touring North America is a series of field guides by leading professional authorities under the auspices of the 1992 International Geographical Congress. These meetings of the International Geographical Union (IGU) have convened every four years for over a century. Field guides of the IGU have become established as significant scholarly contributions to the literature of field analysis. Their significance is that they relate field facts to conceptual frameworks.

Unlike the last Congress in the United States in 1952, which had only four field seminars, the 1992 IGC entails 13 field guides ranging from the low latitudes of the Caribbean to the polar regions of Canada, and from the prehistoric relics of pre-Columbian Mexico to the contemporary megalopolitan eastern United States. Our series also continues the tradition of a transcontinental traverse from the nation's capital to the California coast.

This analysis of the Southern Rocky Mountains and the Colorado Plateau embraces its salient physical and human settlement patterns. It includes the complex evolution of Indian, Hispanic, and Anglo occupants and also the spectacular scenery of the canyonlands and the rugged Rockies.

Cotton Mather, president of the New Mexico Geographical Society, has been an observer and student of the American West for more than 60 years. P. P. Karan, professor of geography at the University of Kentucky, is a recognized international scholar of cultural and economic development. George F. Thompson is president of the Center for American Places.

Anthony R. de Souza
BETHESDA, MARYLAND

◺ Acknowledgments

The authors are grateful to all the good people who participated in the making of this book, some of whom deserve special recognition.

Thomas C. Hunt, Ph.D., a first-rate ecologist and geographer from Madison, Wisconsin, was of great help to us in the field where so much of the primary research was conducted.

Bruce McGee of McGees Gallery in Holbrook, Arizona, and Bill Malone of the Hubbell Trading Post in Ganado, Arizona, provided invaluable information on the historical development of trading posts in Arizona and New Mexico. Bruce, Bill, and their families are true pioneers of the Southwest, and the book has been enriched by their intimate knowledge of the Hopi and Navajo.

John Trujillo of Trujillo's Weaving Shop in Chimayó, New Mexico, shared many fine moments with us on the history of Spanish weaving in the Chimayó community. John is also responsible for spreading the aesthetic value of his art into the finest museums in the United States and Europe.

Teresita Naranjo of Santa Clara Pueblo near Española, New Mexico, is one of the finest human beings and potters around. She has done much to inform the American public—including American Presidents in the White House—of the fine art of Pueblo ceramics, and she was most generous in sharing stories about potters and their family histories for Santa Clara Pueblo and the other Pueblos in the region.

John B. Jackson, a longtime friend and the founder of the famous *Landscape* magazine, is one of the greatest geographical writers the United States has ever produced. Thank goodness he moved from the East to New Mexico following World War II, for, among his many accomplishments as an author and scholar, he has brought to the forefront of American geographical scholarship the value of the cultural heritage of Spanish America. Where would modern geography be without Brinck Jackson's many contributions?

A monumental contribution to the literature of the Southwest comes from Alvar Carlson, professor of geography at Bowling Green State University in Ohio and a longtime student and observer of the region. His book, *The Spanish-American Homeland: Four Centuries in New Mexico's Río Arriba,* is as fine a book on the region as any on the market. It will no doubt be considered a geographical classic within another generation, if not sooner. Of this book, Brinck Jackson writes, "I keep telling visitors and newcomers that they must read it as soon as they can."

David W. Lantis, emeritus professor of geography at California State University, Chico, did his doctoral dissertation on the San Luis Valley, and he remains the authority on the parklands of the Rocky Mountains. Over the years, he has contributed much to our personal understanding of this region, for which we are grateful.

We also acknowledge the work of some dedicated interns at the National Geographic Society who were responsible for producing the maps: Nikolas H. Huffman, cartographic designer for the 27th IGC; Patrick Gaul, GIS specialist at COMSIS in Sacramento, California; Scott Oglesby, who was responsible for the relief artwork; Lynda Barker, Michael B. Shirreffs, and Alisa Pengue Solomon. These interns were assisted by the staff at the National Geographic Society Map Library, Book Collection, Illustrations Library, Cartographic Division, Computer Applications, and Typographic Services. Special thanks go to Susie Friedman of Computer Applications for procuring the hardware needed to finish this project on schedule.

We thank Lynda Sterling, public relations manager and executive assistant to Anthony R. de Souza, the series editor; Natalie Jacobus and Richard Walker for proofreading the volume; Cynthia Suchman for indexing; and Tod Sukontarak for photo research. Purna Makaram at the Center for American Places retyped the manuscript for us.

And many thanks are extended to Kenneth Arnold, director of Rutgers University Press, and to his capable staff, especially Karen Reeds, the science editor who served as an enthusiastic and able liaison between her press in New Brunswick, New Jersey, and Anthony R. de Souza at the National Geographic Society in Washington, D.C.

Last, but not least, it is with a great deal of pleasure that we thank Julie Mather and Hazel Karan, whose involvement in the project was so meaningful. On numerous field outings, they gave us the woman's perspective to the rich and varied regional scene. Their insightful comments and questions were very useful to us as we went about the enjoyable task of reading and interpreting the physical and cultural features of this great regional landscape we call "Beyond the Great Divide."

It was our objective to provide a broad and informative geographical interpretation to this part of the United States, one that would appeal to a wide array of domestic and foreign travelers. We have done our very best to make sure that all factual information herein is accurate and up-to-date, but we know that some errors are inevitable, for which we would like to apologize in advance.

Errors of fact, omission, or interpretation are entirely our responsibility; the opinions and interpretations are not necessarily those of the 27th International Geographical Congress, which is the sponsor of this field guide and the *Touring North America* series.

PART ONE

Introduction to the Region

△ Introduction

Americans have a grand vision that embraces two fundamental components of our land: namely, the East and the West, separated by the Great Divide.

In the East are our nation's capital, and most of our population, most of our private land, most of the cultivation, most of our lowland, most of our factories, most of our roads and old canals, most of our senators, and most of our nation as it was before 1842.

To the West are most of our scantily settled lands, most of our public terrain, most of our rangeland, most of our highland, most of our Indians, most of our park land, and most of our push to incorporate, consolidate, regulate, and subsidize for an enormous fling.

As Americans, we find this inevitable. When we were but thirteen colonies, most of our land and people were on the Eastern Seaboard and Piedmont. Then the Great Divide was the Appalachians, stretching from northern Alabama and Georgia into New England. Our romantic hero was Daniel Boone (b. 1734; d. 1820), to be followed by such colorful characters as Davy Crockett (b. 1786; d. 1836) and Andy Jackson (b. 1767; d. 1845). They pioneered and with them the Great Divide was pushed to the West. So the East was no longer merely on the Atlantic side of the Allegheny Front and the Cumberland Escarpment.

The westward movement continued. The nation's population center shifted steadily across the meridians. Beyond it always was the Great Divide. Long standing on the west bank of the Mississippi River, at Davenport, Iowa, was the sign inscribed "Where the West begins." But the Mississippi was bridged and the push ever onward was to the West. When Walter Prescott Webb's famous book, *The Great Plains,* appeared in 1931, the new line proclaimed as separating the East and the West was that which marked the margin of the timbered eastern region and the treeless Great Plains. The latter was the romantic land of the bison, the cowboy, the windmill, the frontier, and, in the words of John J. Ingalls of Kansas, the "receding horizons . . . born of distance, silence, and solitude."

Decades later the Great Plains region was transformed. The plow had turned the turf, two of the world's greatest wheat belts emerged, oil fields and open-pit coal mines appeared, superhighways were built, irrigation spread, and the rangeland and the cowboy retreated. Denver, a skyscraper metropolis, arose. The Great Divide was no longer the Appalachians, or the Mississippi River, or the margin of the timbered eastern region. Now it was at the Rocky Mountain Front, at the Great Divide.

What is the Great Divide? Historically, it has been the boundary between the settled East and the pioneer West. This, in the chapters of time, has been enumerated by the census and really demarcated by the cartographer.

There are those who bemoan the passing of the frontier. Little do they appreciate that most of our West today is still unoccupied, still a part of the public domain. And, indeed, little do they acknowledge that only just recently, in 1959, more than one-half million square miles of Alaska was transferred into statehood. And Alaska is still mostly an unoccupied land! The frontier is yet with us, in fact. But more important than this is that the ideals and concepts of our society have been implanted and constantly renewed in the pioneer experience in a land far from the Old World and its inherited social institutions. And furthermore, that these ideals and aspirations are ingrained in our souls, and that they will persist long after the last parcel of land has passed from public into private domain.

So, dear traveler, when we proceed up the Rocky Mountain Front, remember that we are not only going from the settled East into the vast and wide open West; far more significant is what this Great Divide means symbolically and to the sustenance of the American spirit.

Denver is close to the western margin of the Great Plains, but it is also the only U.S. metropolis near the base of the Rockies. It is virtually astride the Great Divide. As such, it is a symbolic city as well as an interregional city in function and perspective. It is indeed the Gateway to the West.

DENVER

Much of the guidebook guff on Denver strays far from reality. The city is set not at the very edge of the mountains, but is planted squarely on the Great Plains. The heart of the city is about 15 miles away from the Rocky Mountain Front. Chamber of Commerce publicity photographs depict the snow-capped Rockies towering over the city, a feat neatly accomplished by the distance compression of high-powered telephoto lenses. In addition, you may visit Denver in August when snow is not present even in the mountains.

Denver has problems. Common to every large city in our nation, Denver has severe air pollution at times of high air pressure and atmospheric calm. Additionally, the infrastructure of the city is in dire need of attention, and substandard housing and social malaise characterize large areas—especially in some of the poorer black and Hispanic sections. Problems also affect Denver's satellite settlements. *The Denver Post,* for example, on 24 October 1990, carried a special article reporting that the Adolph Coors Company in Golden pleaded guilty to state water-quality law violations and that the company had agreed to pay $750,000 in fines for releasing carcinogenic chemicals into Clear Creek. Unfortunately, other serious problems exist in and around Denver. One of the most critical concerns water supply. Also, Denver is beset with awesome rush-hour traffic jams and has gridlocks that reach onto the interstate highways.

Denver stubbornly and tirelessly proclaims that its elevation is exactly 1 mile. This assertion is on signs at every major highway entrance to the city, despite the fact that the urban site is obviously

Denver and the Great Plains

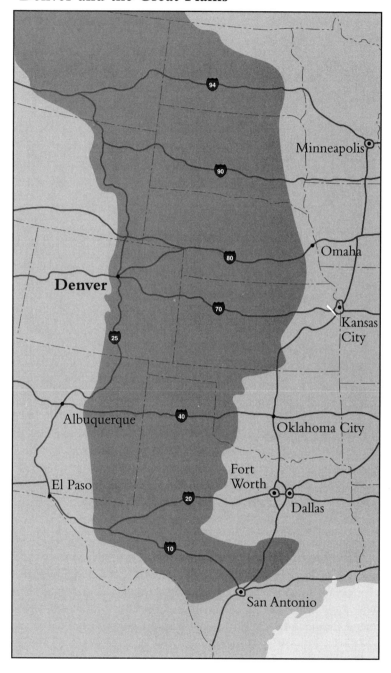

not level. The city is roughly a mile high, but it is nearly 2 miles below the loftiest mountain peaks to the west. Now the advanced ranks of Denver's publicists are asserting that the mile-high elevation is precisely that of the thirteenth step on the west side of the State Capitol—a measurement actually off by a few feet.

Exaggerations aside, Denver is a remarkable city. No other city within 600 miles is so large; its metropolitan population (Denver and suburbs) is 1.9 million. Six interstate highways go east-west across the Great Plains; only one (I-25) goes north-south and that is near the base of the Rockies where I-25, I-70, and I-76 intersect. Denver is that commanding superhighway intersection. Denver, also, is an Amtrak railroad hub. Six trains arrive daily from Los Angeles, San Francisco, Seattle, and Chicago. Important stops for skiers are made at such towns as Winter Park and Glenwood Springs. No other ski area on the continent has so many visitors as the cluster of facilities west of Denver. Skiers come from every quarter of the nation as well as from overseas. Facilitating their travel is Denver's Stapleton International Airport, the fourth busiest in the United States. This airport is overcrowded, so a new one is being constructed. It will be the largest in the world, its fifty square miles larger than the combined area of the Dallas-Fort Worth and Chicago O'Hare airports. The new Denver airport will have 206 gates and 12 runways. The Federal Aviation Administration predicts that it will be the world's second busiest, capable of handling 110 million passengers annually.

The astute traveler will consider experiencing some of Denver's special events. Our favorite is the National Western Stock Show and Rodeo, an annual event in mid-January. This is billed as the world's largest livestock exposition. If you enjoy horse shows, the judging of fine livestock, and seeing real live cowboys perform, this is the very best. But lodging facilities and the famous restaurants are jam-packed then, so make your reservations early. (For information about tickets and events, telephone 303-297-1166.) Other special attractions annually in Denver include the Broncos professional football games at the Mile

High Stadium, capacity 75,000 fanatic fans; the new Colorado Rockies professional baseball games and the Denver Nuggets professional basketball games; the Festival of the Mountain held on Labor Day weekend (telephone 303-295-7900, ext. 102, for information); and, during the first weekend in June, the Cherry Blossom Festival, a Japanese cultural event centered on Sakura Square (telephone 303-295-0304).

The park system of Denver is most unusual. It includes forty-nine municipally-owned mountain areas nearby besides the parks within the city that include the lovely Denver Botanic Gardens, the Platte River Greenway, and Confluence Park. Confluence Park is where the first gold prospectors encamped, and where Denver was born.

Other major attractions are the Museum of Western Art with works of Bierstadt, O'Keeffe, Remington, and Russell; the Corinthian-style state capitol building with its gold-leafed dome; the Denver Center for the Performing Arts; the extraordinary Tattered Cover Bookstore at the Cherry Creek Shopping Center; and the historic Brown Palace Hotel—one of America's finest. (If you cannot afford to lodge at the Brown Palace, remember the tea in the lobby—with sandwiches, scones, and chocolate truffles—served Monday through Saturday at 1400 to 1600.)

Historians emphasize Denver's origin as two rival gold-mining camps: Auraria and Denver City, formally unified in 1860. Denver's first setback came in 1866 when the Union Pacific Railroad announced it would go through Cheyenne, Wyoming, not Denver. By 1870, however, Denver had manipulated a rail connection northward to Cheyenne and had a rail connection eastward on the Kansas Pacific. This was viewed as being linked by rail from coast to coast and to the Great Lakes. Until World War II, Denver's fortune was closely bound to farming and ranching on the plains and to mining ventures in the mountains. After World War II, tourism and high technology industries boomed and vast nearby coal and oil reserves were being exploited. Two thousand energy firms were in the Front Range area by 1980, and Denver had 21,000 energy jobs by 1982. Today, Denver is a major agricultural trade focus; a huge federal regional office center; a tourist hub; a financial, manufacturing, distribution, and transportation core; and a city with a vast surplus of downtown office space. Notwithstanding present and past problems, Denver today is one of the most attractive cities in the United States. Moreover, it is a place par excellence for obtaining maps, travel guides, and other travel provisions.

The Southern Rockies

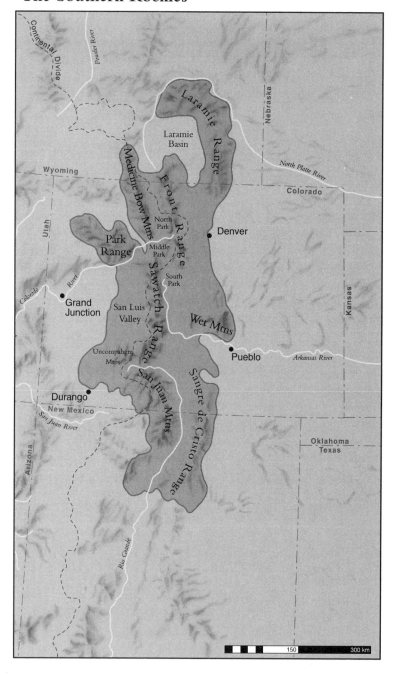

THE SOUTHERN ROCKY MOUNTAINS

COMPONENTS OF NATURE

Landform specialists refer to the Rocky Mountains as a "system," meaning that the numerous ranges of the system are related in age and origin. This system is usually subdivided into six "provinces" which extend over 3,000 miles from the southern end of the Sangre de Cristo Range in north-central New Mexico to the Brooks Range in northern Alaska. The southernmost province, the Southern Rockies, has a length reaching north-south for approximately 420 miles. This province is the highest of the entire mountain system, and it has about fifty peaks exceeding 14,000 feet elevation and culminating in the Sawatch Range at the peaks of Mount Elbert (14,431 feet) and Mount Massive (14,421 feet) in Colorado.

The Southern Rockies consist mainly of two parallel, north-south belts of ranges. The eastern or Front Range, by name, extends from the Cache la Poudre River to the Arkansas River. The same range north of the Cache la Poudre River is referred to as the Laramie Range. South of the Arkansas River, the same fold is known as the Wet Mountains. The western belt is comprised of the Park, Sawatch, and Sangre de Cristo ranges. Associated with these ranges are several irregular ranges such as the San Juan and the Uncompahgre mountains. The two parallel belts are severely eroded, great anticlines (upfolds) with cores of Precambrian (ancient) crystalline rocks that are usually flanked by steeply inclined (younger) sedimentary rocks. The San Juan Mountains, however, are comprised mainly of volcanic materials.

Between the mountain ranges are four large treeless basins, known as "parks." These are North Park (8,300 feet at Walden); Middle Park (7,322 feet at Kremmling); South Park (8,875 feet at Hartsel); and San Luis Park, usually referred to as the San Luis Valley (7,500 feet at Alamosa).

The ancestral Rocky Mountains were formed about 300 million years ago in the Pennsylvanian Period. The present Rocky Mountains are mostly a result of the early Tertiary Period, about sixty million years ago. William Morris Davis (b. 1850; d. 1934), Wallace W. Atwood (b. 1872; d. 1949), and numerous other famed geomorphologists have drawn special attention to the Rocky Mountain Peneplain, an ancient erosion surface which today is a broad, rolling upland mostly at 8,000 to 9,500 feet elevation. In the past, this peneplain extended east to the High Plains surface. Subsequent to its formation, however, a lower erosion level known as the Colorado Piedmont developed.

The Colorado Mineral Belt, with closely spaced faults, is a transverse belt of the Front Range that extends west-southwest from Boulder to Dillon. Most of the mining centers of the Front Range are in this belt.

North and Middle Parks are a synclinal basin, separated by the belt of volcanic rocks called the Rabbit Ears Range, with Cretaceous and Tertiary strata. Most of South Park is a granite peneplain. The San Luis Valley is a structural basin with deep-lying Paleocene (early Tertiary) deposits and later ones on through Quaternary time. This valley and the Arkansas Valley are the north end of a gigantic rift that extends south to southern New Mexico.

Most of the people in the Southern Rockies live in, not upon, the mountains; that is, they live along the major valleys or in the major basins, referred to as parks. From maps you will note that most of the towns are along I-70 and U.S. Highways 24, 40, 50, 160, and 285. These are valley and basin roads, or connections thereto, with considerable ranges in temperatures and precipitation.

The mountain climates and vegetation belts are altitudinal zonations, mainly modified by shelter or exposure. Skiers are quickly

Temperature and Precipitation in the Southern Rocky Mountains

Station	Location	Elevation (in feet)	Average Temperature (Fahrenheit) in January	Average Temperature (Fahrenheit) in July	Average Annual Precipitation (in inches)
Denver, Colorado	Western Great Plains	5,280	32.0	72.5	14.0
Durango, Colorado	Valley, San Juan Mountains	6,505	24.8	67.0	19.5
Idaho Springs, Colorado	Valley, Front Range	7,500	27.0	62.5	15.4
Leadville, Colorado	Valley, Sawatch Range	10,152	17.6	56.2	19.6
Manassa, Colorado	Basin, San Luis Valley	7,700	19.8	62.6	6.7
Salida, Colorado	Valley, Sangre de Cristo Range	7,050	27.6	65.1	11.7
Santa Fe, New Mexico	Foothills, Sangre de Cristo Range	6,996	29.2	68.9	14.2

aware of sunshine and shade contrasts as well as elevational changes in temperature. The vegetation mirrors vividly these conditions. One notes, for example, the lower tree line on northern mountain slopes and the more xerophytic vegetation in the most sheltered valleys and basins. The park known as the San Luis Valley illustrates clearly this altitudinal zonation. In the center of the park are sagebrush, greasewood, and mesquite as well as patches of alkali. Eastward and up the Sangre de Cristo Range, the hiker crosses a belt of steppe grasses and then in successive altitudinal zones a piñon-juniper belt, pine-oak belt, fir-aspen belt, spruce-fir belt, the tree line, and the alpine tundra. At the upper reaches of the forest, the trees are stunted and gnarled under the influence of strong winds. Here one finds the beautiful forms of the bristlecone pine.

The change in altitude per 1,000 feet is often stated to be the environmental equivalent of 600 miles of latitudinal change. Thus, to move from Alamosa, Colorado (7,544 feet), 20 miles eastward and then to the top of Mount Blanca (14,345 feet) is the approximate equivalent of traveling from Alamosa to the North Pole!

SKILAND

The complex of ski resorts in the Southern Rockies exceeds that of any other ski region in the United States or Canada. Vail and Aspen are world-class ski resorts, and the World Alpine Ski Championships were hosted at Vail in 1989. European skiers are now flocking to Colorado, and the number of European visitors to Colorado surged upward 47 percent after the world event at Vail. Ski packages to Colorado are attractive in both price and quality. The cost of renting a condominium in Colorado is lower than a hotel room in Switzerland. The annual number of lift tickets in the 1980s in Colorado increased from fewer than six million to almost ten million. The United States is now challenging Europe as a world leader in skiing. The number of Japanese skiers is small, but increasing dramatically. Japanese tour companies are featuring Vail and Aspen in their tour promotions. In addition, Breckenridge and Steamboat Springs have Japanese-owned resorts.

Twelve million Americans ski, and many more persons accompany them as tagalongs. In addition, many people are employed in transporting, feeding, housing, and entertaining these vacationers. So ski business is big business. The highest mountain in the Far West is California's Mount Whitney (14,494 feet), but about fifty of Colorado's peaks are higher than 14,000 feet and they are 700 miles closer to the highly populated eastern United States. Small wonder that more skiers come to this region and come via Denver with its commanding interstate highway intersection and its superb airline and rail connections.

The ski business is fast changing. Twenty-five years ago, in the pioneer stage, the ski image was of blonde coeds and Nordic jocks sweeping down the snowy slopes. Then there were about 1,400 ski areas in the United States. Now, through consolidation, the total is near 500 megaresorts.

Kennard E. Smith (b. 1946), a leading U.S. geographer in the business world, wrote his doctoral dissertation on skiing. He reports major changes in the ski industry: the growth of "megaresorts" at the expense of smaller ski areas; the growing proportion of older people as skiers; and the increasing popularity of cross-country skiing. Colorado has maintained cross-country trails that are accessible with payment of a small trail fee.

Snow-making equipment has expanded the area and the season of skiing. The Colorado Rockies ski region has enhanced both its lead nationally and its facilities with this addition to the ski industry. Colorado's ski season now extends from November to April with a peak between Christmas and New Year's Day. (For further information on downhill skiing, write Colorado Ski Country USA, One Civic Center Plaza, 1560 Broadway Drive, Suite 1440, Denver, Colorado 80202, U.S.A. or telephone 303-837-0793. For information on cross-country skiing, write Colorado Cross-Country Ski Association, P.O. Box 169, Winter Park, Colorado 80482, U.S.A. or telephone 303-887-2152.)

Snowmobiling is increasingly popular and most of the National Forest land is available for this kind of recreation. (Contact the

District Ranger, Forest Supervisor, or Regional Office for their general recreation maps.) Snowmobilers are cautioned about numerous hazards, including hypothermia, altitude sickness, and snow avalanches.

Hypothermia is caused by exposure to cold, often aggravated by wetness, wind, and exhaustion. Hypothermia is the chief killer of outdoor recreationists.

Altitude sickness may affect some persons at elevations as low as 8,000 feet. Symptoms may be headache, nausea, dizziness, breathlessness, loss of appetite, and severe fatigue. Gradual ascent, a high carbohydrate diet, prevention of dehydration, and reduced physical exertion are advised for those unaccustomed to high altitudes.

Avalanches are a major hazard to both winter travelers and recreationists, and no one can predict them with accuracy. The two principal types of avalanches are loose snow and slab avalanches. The former type moves with little internal cohesion, as a formless mass. The slab avalanche involves a large mass of snow that begins to move at once. Avalanches are most common on 30- to 45-degree slopes and may occur on short or long slopes. Natural obstructions, such as large rocks and trees, help anchor snow. However, avalanches can start even in tree areas. The safest routes are ridgetops and on windward slopes. (The Colorado Avalanche Information Center has avalanche hazard forecasts available from mid-November through April. Near Aspen, telephone 303-920-1664; near Denver, telephone 303-236-9435.)

RIDING HIGH AND THE WATER DIVIDE

Touring the Southern Rocky Mountains takes the traveler over the highest automobile passes anywhere in the United States or Canada. California's vaunted Tioga Pass (9,945 feet) at the eastern boundary of Yosemite National Park is surpassed by numerous high passes in the Southern Rockies. These high passes extend from Snowy Range Pass (10,800 feet) in the Medicine Bow Mountains 40 miles west of Laramie, Wyoming, to the Cumbres Pass (10,022 feet) in the San Juan Mountains 8 miles northeast of Chama, New Mexico. The highest of all automobile passes in the United States is Independence Pass (12,095 feet) just east of Aspen, Colorado. The entrance to the Eisenhower Memorial Tunnel on I-70, 25 miles west of Idaho Springs, Colorado, is at 11,013 feet elevation; this is under Loveland Pass (11,992 feet), which was formerly used by U.S. Highway 6 traffic. Other high passes include Fall River Pass (11,796 feet) in Rocky Mountain National Park and Berthoud Pass (11,314 feet) about 22 miles west of Idaho Springs.

Persons wishing to go really sky-high might consider driving to the top of Pikes Peak (14,110 feet). It is 19 miles upgrade from the toll gate (7,309 feet). The road is open June 1 to August 31, and from May to October *if* weather permits. The drive is hard on your car and hard on the driver who must make 156 turns enroute. The easiest way to the summit, however, is to take the cog railway from 515 Ruxton Avenue, Manitou Springs (a suburb of Colorado Springs); it is a three-hour trip. Reservations are required (telephone 719-685-5401), and it is open May through October, snow conditions permitting. From the summit one can actually see 100 miles south to New Mexico and 75 miles north to Denver. A tourist advisory suggests that a swimming suit is less suitable for this Pikes Peak jaunt than a warm jacket. It is a cold fact that snow flurries may be encountered in any summer month at these high elevations.

All of the highest mountain passes of the Southern Rockies are along or near the Continental Divide. This divide, not to be confused with the Great Divide discussed earlier, separates drainage to the Atlantic Ocean from that to the Pacific Ocean. Three significant rivers of the continent have their headwaters in Colorado at the Continental Divide. These are the Colorado River, which flows into the Pacific, and the Arkansas River and the Rio Grande, which flow to the Gulf of Mexico, an arm of the Atlantic. Years ago, this all seemed merely interesting. Now, the waters of these rivers are subject to high-stakes legal battles intrastate, interstate, and internationally.

The state of Colorado needs more water. Its population and per capita water use have expanded markedly. Most of the people and most of the water consumption are east of the mountains; most of the source of the state's water in on the "West Slope." Eastern Coloradoans want to use the water while western Coloradoans cling to it for future use. The struggle, however, has greater dimensions.

Colorado River water is used by all the states down the drainage system, particularly California and Arizona. But some of it, by international compact, is allocated to Mexico. So all these parties are in the contest for Colorado River water.

Arkansas River water is in an analogous struggle within the state of Colorado, between the people in eastern Colorado and western Colorado. Furthermore, the Arkansas Valley is one of only two irrigated strips that completely stretches across the Great Plains. So the waters of this river, also, are in interstate contention.

The Rio Grande—known to Mexicans as the Río Bravo del Norte—water is used for irrigation in Colorado, New Mexico, and Texas. Moreover, the Rio Grande irrigates lands in both Mexico and the United States, However, much of the lower Rio Grande water used on the American side of the border has its source from Mexican tributaries. This situation has forced the Americans to take a broader perspective in the allocation of waters from both the Rio Grande and the Colorado River.

Intensified demands for water have involved the transfer of water rights of private property, tunneling water through mountains, and focusing upon artesian supplies. Larger urban centers have purchased ranches, for example, just to obtain the water rights of those properties. Borings have been made through mountains to divert water from the West Slope under the Continental Divide. The Frying Pan Project diverts water from the Frying Pan and Roaring Fork tributaries of the Colorado River under the Continental Divide to the upper Arkansas River. Also, the Colorado-Big Thompson Project tunnels water for 13 miles under the Continental Divide from the Colorado River headwaters into the east-flowing Big Thompson River. The San Luis Valley, the major agricultural area in the Southern Rocky Mountains, is famous for its artesian water supply and for its high-ground water table, which provides for some subirrigation. Until now, most of the effort has been to secure more water, not to use it more wisely.

THE TREELESS BASINS

The largest areas of settlement in the Colorado Rockies are the parks, or treeless basins. North, Middle, and South parks are almost entirely in privately owned land used for hay or the grazing of cattle. Cattle ranching has reigned supreme in these three parks, and until recently the towns there were simply small trade centers for the ranching communities.

Most of the highlands surrounding the parks are in national forests; that is, land in the public domain. These national forests, however, contain extensive areas used for summer grazing. In the early years of cattle ranching, the cattle were in the parks in the winter and moved freely into the highlands in summer. After the federal government established national forests in 1891, however, the ranchers had to obtain rental permits for this summer pasturage. The government has regulated this carefully and has gradually reduced the number of livestock units permitted on these summer pastures. Since most operations were modest family ranches and summer pasturage became increasingly constricted, many ranchers turned to registered pure-bred livestock operations to maintain economic viability. With further reduction of federal grazing permits, economics forced numerous ranchers to resort to dude or recreational ranch operations or to lease rights for hunting and fishing, and recreational phases have become vital aspects of the ranching economy. This is clearly evident in the main towns. These towns are Walden (population 1,000) in North Park; Kremmling (population 1,400) in Middle Park; and Fairplay (population 500) in South Park. The same is true in the ranching area of the upper Arkansas Valley in the towns of Buena Vista (population 2,200) and Salida (population 5,000).

Public pressure—mainly pleas for protecting watersheds, increasing wildlife, and diversifying recreational goals—motivated gradual federal reduction of livestock-grazing permits. Deer, elk, and antelope graze on the same forage as cattle, so, as the number of cattle diminished, the number of deer, elk, and antelope increased. Which is more valuable, an antelope or a yearling steer? To a vegetarian, the answer is simple.

The San Luis Valley is the largest and most complex of the treeless basins known as parks. This park is 125 miles long and has an average width of 50 miles. White settlement began about 1850 and grew rapidly with the gold discoveries in the 1870s. Ranching is important, but there is much irrigated agriculture. Irrigation from the Rio Grande and from more than 7,000 artesian wells water fields of potatoes, barley, wheat, alfalfa, and hardy vegetables. Some sections are also subirrigated. Alamosa (population 8,000) and Monte Vista (population 4,000) are the two large towns in the park. The composition of population in the San Luis Valley is diverse. It includes the old Spanish settlement of San Luis, descendants of Mormon immigrants from Alabama and Georgia, and migrants from the Middle West. Unlike North, Middle, and South parks, many ranchers in the San Luis Valley raise both sheep and cattle. Transhumance is the normal pattern: livestock graze on government highland pasture in summer and are moved to privately owned lands of the San Luis Valley during colder months.

THE RÍO ARRIBA

The Río Arriba is one of the oldest and most distinctive cultural regions in the United States, encompassing about 20,000 square miles. It is the Spanish-American homeland in the upper Rio Grande Valley and its tributary valleys in the Rocky Mountains of New Mexico. When the Spanish first settled this area nearly four

Rio Arriba

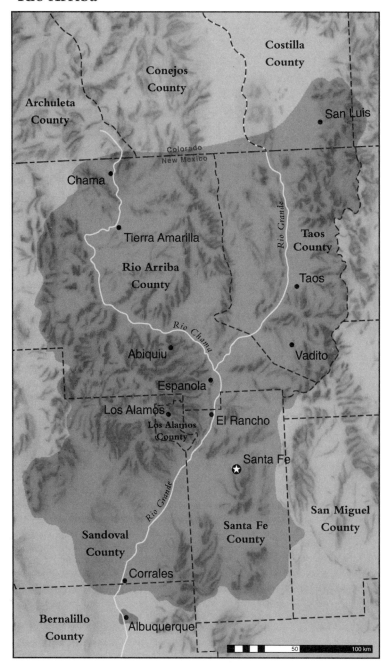

centuries ago in 1598, there was already a highly developed Pueblo Indian civilization. Anglos arrived later. These three numerically important cultural groups—Indian, Hispanic, Anglo—have developed a culture distinct from the rest of the United States in its food, architecture, and mode of life. This is the only region in the United States where cultural effacement was not the product of Anglo occupance, and the only region where new residents fall under a regional spell, where they do not so much change the region as the region changes them.

The Pueblo Indians built agglomerated settlements comprised of compact, many-chambered, flat-roofed, adobe structures built around plazas. Their culture strongly contrasted with that of the nomadic or semi-nomadic Apache and Navajo Indians. Among the Pueblo Indians, agriculture, including fruit raising, was highly developed, and they sustained population concentrations with a highly structured social organization and significant arts and crafts.

The Spanish, who came north from Mexico, formally occupied this region, and the Indian country was subdivided into ecclesiastical districts. New aspects were introduced, but some of the oid were retained. The process was further moderated with the coming of the Anglos. So today, for example, Indian languages, Spanish, and English are all spoken in the region. And architecture known as the "Santa Fe Style" is basically that of the Pueblo Indians— made of adobe, with flat roofs supported by wooden beams called *vigas*. The Spanish modified the construction method by bricking the adobe, sometimes placing wrought iron over the windows, and using carved wooden doors. The Anglos added technology in the sanitary, lighting, and cooking systems. But "Santa Fe Style" is an illustration of a fusion of three cultures that characterize so many aspects of Río Arriba.

The four urban centers that dominate Río Arriba are Santa Fe (population 88,000), Los Alamos (population 11,650), Taos (population 4,230), and Española (population 7,340). Santa Fe is the social and political capital. Taos is a curious complex of the Indian Pueblo, the Spanish community, and the Anglos in the world of art and literature in addition to the hordes of winter skiers. Los Alamos is the huge nuclear research center, a major employer of scientists in residence plus droves of commuting Indians and Spanish workers. Nearly central to Santa Fe, Taos, and Los Alamos is the blue-collar town of Española. Española has three Indian Pueblos in its immediate environs—San Ildefonso, San Juan, Santa Clara—and is focal to many small Spanish-American communities in the tributary valleys of the Rio Grande. These communities are set in dissected highlands with small enclaves of gentle topography that remain largely secluded from mainstream America.

The Colorado Plateau

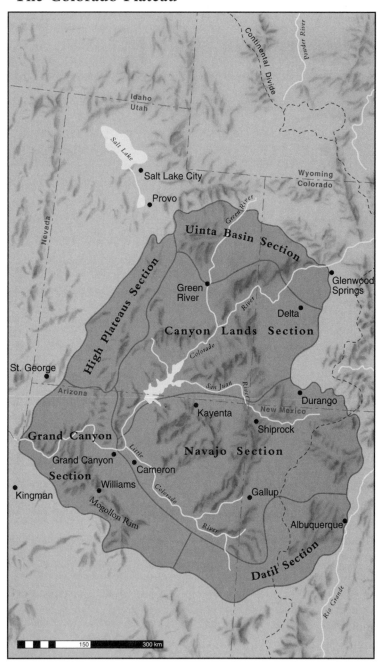

THE COLORADO PLATEAU

ITS FUNDAMENT

The Colorado Plateau includes much of the four states of Arizona, Colorado, New Mexico, and Utah. Many people refer to this region as the Four Corners Area, where indeed the four state boundaries intersect at a point about 70 miles east of the region's center.

The region (130,000 square miles) is considerably larger than either the United Kingdom or Italy, yet it contains far fewer people than Rhode Island or the combined populations of Greenland, Iceland, and Kuwait. Statisticians report that vast areas of the Colorado Plateau contain less than one-tenth of a human being per square mile. (We have explored this region over the past half century and have encountered only one human being for every ten square miles.) Field observation reveals that most of the region has no resident population. It is simply devoid of human beings except for perhaps a lone cowboy, Indian, or wayfarer wending his or her way across arroyos, around buttes and mesas, avoiding precipitous canyons, traversing lava fields, sometimes going through tall forest, then over tawny stretches of short grass that are rarely succulent, encountering few water holes but many prairie dogs, and then surmounting yonder horizon to suddenly view one of the greatest sights in our universe—a grand canyon, the "Great Goosenecks" of the San Juan River, the awesome columns of Monument Valley, or giant, natural arches of rock transcending space. No other region in the United States has such exotic natural landscapes, so ethereal in form and color that one wonders if this is on the planet Earth. Yet this is the Colorado Plateau, the home of an ancient civilization, the Anasazi. But it is the least known part of the forty-eight contiguous states. As J. Russell Smith (b. 1874; d. 1966)—perhaps the best regional geographer the United States has ever produced—stated in 1925 in his famous book, *North America,* "it was only in 1909 that the first white man saw the greatest natural bridge in the world, the Rainbow Bridge in southeastern Utah."

The major physical characteristics of the Colorado Plateau are: (1) its elevated position, mostly 5,000 to 11,000 feet; (2) the approximate horizontality of its stratified rocks; (3) the presence of hundreds of deep canyons, including the Grand Canyon; (4) the rock structural control of most landform features—basins, upwards, and faults; (5) the angularity of most of the landforms; (6) the eruptive igneous features and lava flows that cover about 15,000 square miles; (7) the altitudinal zonation of vegetation from sagebrush and greasewood at lowest levels to spruce and alpine shrub at highest levels, with more than half of the area in forest; (8) the great thermal range annually in each altitudinal zone, plus the deep snows over much of the region in winter; and (9) the near-complete (about 90 percent) drainage of the area by the Colorado River and its tributaries.

The Colorado Plateau is bordered on the north and east by the higher Rocky Mountains, while the lower Basin and Range Province of horsts (upthrust blocks) and grabens (downdropped blocks) borders the Colorado Plateau on the south and west.

Within the Colorado Plateau are subdivisions with significant areal contrasts.

The Grand Canyon Section is the most spectacular and intricate incisement of the Colorado River. This is bounded by high, fault-block plateaus on the north.

The High Plateaus Section of Utah has a series of north-south trending plateaus which are 9,000 to 11,000 feet (or higher) in elevation. Some of these are lava-capped.

Plant Indicators and Altitudinal Zonation on the Colorado Plateau

Approximate Elevation (in feet)	Common Plants
4,500 to 5,500	Greasewood *(Sarcobatus vermiculatus)*
	Big or common sagebrush *(Artemisia tridentata nutt.)*
	Old man or sand sagebrush *(Artemisia filifolia torr.)*
5,500 to 6,500	Utah juniper *(Juniperus osteosperma torr. [little])*
	Piñon pine *(Pinus cembroides, P. edulis, P. monophylla, P. parryana)*
6,500 to 8,000	Ponderosa pine *(Pinus ponderosa;* also known as western yellow or bull pine)
8,000 to 9,500	Aspen *(Populus tremuloides michx.;* also known as quaking aspen)
	Douglas fir *(Pseudotsuga taxifolia)*
9,500 to 11,000	Engelmann spruce *(Picea engelmannii)*
Above 11,000	Alpine tundra (scant vegetation above the timberline, including dwarf flowers, flowering dwarf herbs, mosses, lichen)

The Uinta Basin Section, abutted on the north by the Uinta Mountains, ranges from about 5,000 to 10,000 feet. Its interior is lower than the periphery, both topographically and structurally.

The Canyon Lands Section, in the central part of the Colorado Plateau, includes the Henry Mountains (huge laccoliths, laccoliths being subterranean lenticular igneous masses that have forced overlying rock upwards), Monument Valley, and many canyons, including those of the Colorado, San Juan, and Green rivers. The spectacular, incised meanders, or "Great Goosenecks," of the San Juan River are in this section.

The Navajo Section, between the San Juan and Little Colorado rivers, is an area of fewer and not so deep canyons. It has scattered volcanic necks, dikes, cones, lava flows, and valuable coal strata. In the Datil Section, in the southeast, are lava flows, lava-capped mesas and buttes, the Mount Taylor volcanic field, and, southeast of Gallup, New Mexico, the Zuni Mountains upward. Visible over great distances are some of the volcanic fields. These include San Francisco Mountain, locally referred to as the San Francisco Peaks (San Francisco Mountain has been sculptured into three summits: Humphreys Peak, Agassiz Peak, and Fremont Peak; the elevation of the former is 12,670 feet, the highest elevation in Arizona), and the Mount Taylor field. The famous Shiprock, in northwestern New Mexico, is a volcanic neck.

On the Colorado Plateau plant indicators of altitudinal zonation vary locally with moisture, soil, and exposure.

THE INDIANS

The Colorado Plateau might also be called Indian Country, for it has been home to the Anasazi, the Pueblo Indians, the Navajo and the Apache, and, to a lesser extent, the Utes.

The Anasazi

The Anasazi, or "ancient ones," were early occupants of the Colorado Plateau. They came from Asia, and from about 7000 to 200 BC were living by hunting small game and gathering edible plants, nuts, seeds, and fruit. By AD 700 to 900, pithouse villages were giving way to aboveground pueblos, cotton had come into use, and the pithouse had become a *kiva,* or ceremonial chamber. By the AD 1100 to 1300 period, the Anasazi population had greatly expanded, agriculture had advanced, cliff dwellings were in use, and a complex socio-religious organization had evolved. This was the

Great Pueblo Period in which trade reached as far as southern Mexico. But during this AD 1100 to 1300 period, environmental problems were emerging, including the depletion of wood and building supplies, soil erosion and arroyos deepening, and the serious drought of 1276 to 1299. This induced emigration from great Anasazi centers, such as those at Mesa Verde and Chaco Canyon, to the Hopi Mesas, the Little Colorado River, the Zuni Mountains, and the Rio Grande Valley.

The Anasazi were the progenitors of Pueblo culture; they were advanced in arts, crafts, and architecture. Most admired in their arts and crafts are their ceramics. Their architecture culminated in multistoried complexes in Mesa Verde and Chaco Canyon. Pueblo Bonito, in Chaco Canyon, had 800 rooms and many kivas! The Cliff Palace at Mesa Verde, one of the largest cliff dwellings in the Southwest, had over 200 rooms. The rudiments of modern "Santa Fe Style" architecture, both structurally and aesthetically, were initiated by Anasazi builders, not by modern-day architects.

Chaco Canyon, today, has two access roads. Both are difficult and avoided by most tourists. (An improved road is being considered.) Mesa Verde, in contrast, is considered as the most spectacular of all Indian ruins in the United States and it is the most popular. A visit to Mesa Verde combines great archeology and attractive scenery. The park is open year round, but the campground is open only from June 1 through September. (For detailed information, write Mesa Verde National Park, Colorado 81330, U.S.A. or telephone 303-529-4465.)

The Pueblo Indians

The Pueblo Indians, or village dwellers, are today divided between those on the Colorado Plateau—the Western Pueblos—and those in the Rio Grande Valley—the Eastern Pueblos. The four Western Pueblo Indians (population on reservations, approximately 27,000) are the Acoma, Hopi, Laguna, and Zuñi. The sixteen Eastern Pueblos (population on reservations, approximately 17,000) are the Cochiti, Isleta, Jemez, Nambe, Picurís, Pojoaque, San Felipe, San Ildefonso, San Juan, Sandia, Santa Ana, Santa Clara, Santo Domingo, Taos, Tesuque, and Zia. The Eastern Pueblos are sometimes referred to as the Rio Grande Pueblos.

The Pueblo Indians speak dialects of several languages. *Tewa* is spoken by Indians at Nambe, Pojoaque, San Ildefonso, San Juan, Santa Clara, and Tesuque Pueblos. It is also the language of Hano village in the Hopi country. *Tiwa* is the language of the Isleta, Picurís, Sandia, and Taos Pueblos. *Keres* is spoken in the Acoma, Cochiti, Jemez, Laguna, San Felipe, Santa Ana, Santo Domingo, and Zia Pueblos. Excluding those at Hano village, the Hopis speak a Uto-Aztecan language. Zuñi Indians speak a language derived from Penutian stock.

The Pueblo Indians have for centuries been a sedentary society, living in villages, with nearby gardens and fields tended by both women and men. The Spanish divided the Pueblo country into ecclesiastical districts, and a Roman Catholic priest was placed in charge of each. The Indians were forced to acknowledge allegiance to the Spanish crown and to the Roman Catholic church. But all was not congenial because the Spanish imposed social changes and encroached on Indian lands. The Pueblo Indians of New Mexico revolted in 1680 and drove the Spanish away; but, in 1692, the Spanish reconquered them.

The Pueblo Indians have been beset with great change since the mid-twentieth century. Highways and television sets have expanded the Pueblo world, bringing the outside in and taking the inside out. This has meant the incursion of tourists, the expansion of social contacts, the decline of Pueblo fields and gardens in favor of chain foodstores; the acquisition of cars and pickup trucks; employment in factories, towns, or the Los Alamos complex; more marriage outside their society; an altered family role; new responsibilities in governance; technological innovations in the kitchen and the bathroom; new ideas in house architecture and town morphology; and engagement in a more complex social net. Indian cultures in North America are strikingly diverse. Compared with other Indian societies, the Pueblo Indians are remarkably successful in maintaining vital elements in their culture, in retaining a strong identity, in adapting to technological change, and in making unique contributions to the American scene.

The Navajo and the Apache

The Navajo and the Apache, members of the Athabascan linguistic stock, migrated from Asia across the Bering Strait. Most of them moved southward over the Great Plains, but near the edge of the Rocky Mountains. Some bands then moved westward, from what is now southern Colorado, through mountain passes and arrived about AD 1500 in the upper San Juan River country.

The nomadic people adjusted their movements to seasonal fluctuations that affected hunting and gathering. Their activity was somewhat modified by adding to their economy corn raising, which had been acquired through contact with Pueblo Indians. The usual Navajo house type was the round or nearly circular hogan (pronounced ho-gan, not ho-gun), derived from Asia. From contact with the Spanish, the Navajo acquired sheep, goats, cattle, and horses and became pastoralists.

The Navajo and the Apache were in frequent conflict with Pueblo Indians, the Spanish, and the Americans. They plundered Pueblo settlements in times of stress, and had various confrontations with the Spanish. Relations with the Americans were hardly amicable, and the California gold rush brought further conflict with Americans who were crossing the Southwest. Treaties were repeatedly made and violated.

Colonel Christopher (Kit) Carson (b. 1809; d. 1868) of Taos, New Mexico, and his troops rounded up 8,354 Navajo and 405 Apache and forced them on the "Long Walk." Others eluded the roundup. The journey began at Fort Defiance, Arizona (established in 1851 a few miles north of Window Rock; nothing remains of the fort today), and continued across the Colorado Plateau country, through the Southern Rocky Mountains, and onward to Fort Sumner (established in 1862 southeast of Las Vegas; presently a state monument) on the Great Plains of New Mexico. Those who did not die on the 400-mile march arrived in December of 1864. By resettlement, the government hoped to transmute these Indians from raiders to peaceful farmers like the Pueblo Indians. The result was a miserable failure. In 1868, a new treaty was signed which established a three-and-one-half million-acre Navajo reservation back upon the Colorado Plateau. Over time this reservation has been enlarged to sixteen million acres (about 25,000 square miles, or about half the size of Alabama or Wisconsin or Iowa or Illinois or Florida), mostly in northeastern Arizona, but with some overlap into New Mexico and Utah. Currently, about fifty-five square miles are dry-farmed, and some additional is irrigated. However, most of the reservation is in pasture, woodland, or mineral exploitation. The Navajo tribe is the largest Indian tribe in the United States, with a reservation population of about 156,000, and a fecundity that keeps the Navajo population remarkably youthful.

The Apache, culturally similar to the Navajo, formerly roamed extensively from the Pecos River to the Colorado River and southward into the Mexican states of Chihuahua and Sonora. Today, the two main groups of Apache in Arizona and New Mexico are the Chiricahua-Mescalero Apache and the Jicarilla. The former (population 2,600) are concentrated on a 460,000-acre reservation in the Sacramento Mountains of the Basin and Range Province, 200 miles southeast of Albuquerque, New Mexico. The Jicarilla (population 2,500) inhabit a reservation of nearly 750,000 acres in the easternmost part of the Colorado Plateau, about 90 miles northwest of Santa Fe. The Jicarilla own many sheep and cattle, and many gas and oil wells, and nearly 300 of them are on the federal payroll. Their reservation management program is exemplary.

The Navajo and the Apache emphasize the importance of the individual, not of the group as is the cultural characteristic of the Pueblo Indians. Another longtime contrast was that Pueblo Indians lived in compact communities, whereas the Navajo and the Apache lived in dispersed, extended family clusters. The modern mode, however, is for Indians in this part of the Southwest to move to urban places. This shift has contributed to population growth in larger off-reservation places such as Gallup, New Mexico, but also at points such as Tuba City, Arizona, which, until recently, were just crossroad clusters.

The enumeration of Indians in the United States is a complex social matter. It was not fashionable earlier in this century to be an Indian; so many Indians "passed" as Hispanic or white. Now, however, it is quite popular to be an American Indian. This sociological change is reflected in an official tripling of the national total of Indians from the 1960 to the 1990 census.

Conservative estimates of the Indian population in 1492 in what is now U.S. territory totaled about four million. Conflict and disease reduced this to about a quarter million by 1890. The population has risen since then to a current total of about 1.8 million, including those who live off reservation lands.

The Ute

The Ute Indians, belonging to the Shoshonean linguistic stock, are present in the Colorado Plateau only in small numbers. The principal bands of the Utes still in existence—several thousand of them—are the Uinta, the Uncompahgre, and the Yampa in western Colorado and eastern Utah, with those on reservations deriving income from oil and gas leases, farming, cattle-raising, and tourism. Prior to the coming of Europeans, the Utes ranged as far south as New Mexico and Arizona, menacing and sometimes destroying the towns of Pueblo Indians and selling their captives into slavery. The Utes had a reputation for being fierce, and their material culture can be said to be inferior to that of the Pueblo Indians, who were sophisticated farmers, artisans, and architects. The Utes were nomadic and did not occupy permanent settlements as did the Pueblo Indians, preferring to live in tepees, which were frequently decorated with brilliantly colored paintings, or in brush or sod shelters.

Utah, of course, took its name from the Utes. In southeastern Utah, Utes have become embroiled in controversial oil rights. Petroleum is present in this part of the Colorado Plateau.

REGIONAL CONSIDERATIONS

When one thinks of the regional considerations of the Colorado Plateau, other than the Indians and its physical characteristics, one quickly focuses on the great scientific surveys of the nineteenth century and the significant role the federal government has had in the region's landholdings.

The Great Surveys

Scientific interest in the Southwest and Interior West has been long-standing. How to conquer it, how to parcel it out, how to use and manage it have been among the key regional considerations.

From the Mexican War (1846 to 1848), the United States gained a half-million square miles (the equivalent of five Colorados, or three Californias, or about one Alaska), including all of the Colorado Plateau. But there were no railroads in the region, and it was imperative for both private and governmental interests to link the settled East and California with reliable transportation. In the effort to achieve this objective, Jefferson Davis (b. 1808; d. 1889), secretary of war in the Cabinet of President Franklin Pierce and later president of the Confederate States of America, obtained a congressional appropriation of $30,000 to purchase two loads of camels for the Army in the Southwest. The supplies were slow in reaching the forts in those days, and "ships of the desert" were conceived as the answer. Camels, acquired in the 1850s from Izmir (Smyrna) in Turkey, were soon displaced by the railroad.

Jefferson Davis also encouraged the Pacific Railroad Surveys. After the Civil War, pressure mounted for more knowledge of the West and four great geographical and geological surveys were conducted from 1867 to 1879. These surveys—headed by Clarence King (b. 1842; d. 1901), George M. Wheeler (b. 1842; d. 1905), Ferdinand V. Hayden (b. 1829; d. 1887), and John Wesley Powell (b. 1834; d. 1902)—are often referred to as "The Great

CAMELS IN THE WEST

North America may well be the original home of the camel. An ancient form of camel, found in Eocene rocks, is barely larger than a jackrabbit, but later specimens, as large as sheep, have a llama-like conformation. On 3 March 1855, the U.S. Congress appropriated $30,000 (a significant amount in those days) for the purchase of camels, presumably of post-Eocene type, to be used for military purposes. Seventy-eight camels were acquired in Turkey and Egypt, including three that perished on the 92-day ship voyage plus two fine camels that were presented by Bey Mohammed Pasha of Egypt. Six Arabs and a Turk were employed to care for the animals aboard the ship. The camels were landed at Indianola, Texas; one load arrived on 14 May 1856 and the other on 10 February 1857.

Lt. Edward F. Beale, "a pioneer in the path of empire," had read M. Huc's two volumes, *Recollections of a Journey through Tartary, Thibet, and China, during the Years 1844, 1845, and 1846* (Appleton, 1852). Lt. Beale was impressed by Huc's praise of the camel for commerce and travel. He used the War Department's imported camels for opening a wagon road to California from Fort Defiance (which had been constructed in 1851 a few miles north of present-day Window Rock, Arizona, to guard the western Navajo country). The railroads, however, soon displaced the use of camels and Lt. Beale was appointed minister to Austria-Hungary.

On 9 September 1863, the War Department (now referred to as the Department of Defense) in Washington, D.C., ordered the camels in California to be sold. Away from Washington, there were circuses and zoos which obtained some of these camels. In addition, some were moved as waste disposal into Mexico and some headed southwest on foot in the direction of Egypt and Turkey. All of them have not been accounted for, of course, but scholars note that, while camel's milk is a welcome addition to coffee, camel meat is reported to be as good as beef. This fact alone may be reason enough for the federal government in Washington to become involved once again with camels in the West.

Surveys." These surveys were made by parties of scientists, photographers, painters, and journalists.

The survey reports of John Wesley Powell and his two associates, Grove Karl Gilbert (b. 1843; d. 1918) and Clarence E. Dutton (b. 1841; d. 1912), made major contributions to our understanding of the West. They, also, laid much of the foundations for our modern science of physiography. Gilbert's "Report on the Geology of the Henry Mountains" *(U.S. Geographical and Geological Survey of the Rocky Mountain Region,* Washington, D.C., 1877) and Dutton's "Report on the Geology of the High Plateaus of Utah" *(U.S. Geographical and Geological Survey of the Rocky Mountain Region,* Washington, D.C., 1880) are genuine scientific classics. Powell's survey included the work of John K. (Jack) Hillers (b. 1843; d. 1925), who left thousands of priceless Indian photographs, and Thomas Moran (b. 1837; d. 1926), the famous landscape painter. Powell's *Exploration of the Colorado River of the West* (43rd Congress, 1st Session, House Miscellaneous Document 300, Washington, D.C., 1875) is a great true adventure story of the one-armed Powell (he lost it in the Civil War) and his party floating down one of the world's most turbulent rivers. It should be read by every youngster in the United States, and by every adult who still retains any red corpuscles. Powell, a great geologist and a capable ethnologist, should be remembered, too, for his *Report on the Lands of the Arid Region of the United States* (Washington, D.C., 1879). This report indicated the hazards of unprincipled exploitation and advocated scientific land classification and governmental regulation of a "general plan" involving new economic, social, and political organization and new concepts of law. His plan would have discarded the rectangular cadastral survey, eliminated the standard size homestead, tied water rights to land titles, redrawn political boundaries to be in harmony with natural conditions, and set aside areas unsuitable for agriculture. That report of over a century ago is still way ahead of its time!

The Landholders

The federal government owns most of the land in the American West. Well over 50 percent of the land from the eastern base of the Rocky Mountains to the Pacific Ocean is in national forests, national parks, national recreational areas, national monuments, national wildlife refuges, national grasslands, national historic parks, national rivers, wildlife management areas, Bureau of Land Management areas, Air Force ranges, Indian reservations, or in some other publicly managed area.

The role of the federal government is particularly pronounced on the Colorado Plateau. For example, approximately one of every five acres in this vast region is in the single reservation of the Navajo Indians. Moreover, the federal government owns more than 90 percent of the commercial forests in Arizona, the state with the largest share of the Colorado Plateau.

The Colorado Plateau long remained a little known region. Deep snow in winter impeded travel. Huge canyons were too broad to span and road construction was retarded. Vast unpopulated areas were without travel provisions, sources of water were undeveloped, and the Indians seemed strange and formidable. Eventually, however, the barriers were breached. A railroad was completed across the southern part of the region in the early 1880s, but automobile traffic did not become important until the 1920s. The legendary highway U.S. 66 (parts of it are still intact) crossed the Plateau, and branch roads afforded tourists access to scenic wonders of the region. Urban centers on the Plateau along Interstate Highway 40, the route of old U.S. 66, are bustling now with truck and tourist traffic (for example, Holbrook, Arizona).

Many affluent desert dwellers to the south are building second homes on the southern rim (Mogollon Rim) of the Plateau.

Great dams have been constructed and lakes formed at taxpayer's expense. Lake Mead on the Arizona-Nevada border, impounded by Hoover Dam, has a shoreline of 550 miles and extends 150 miles into colorful canyons of the Colorado River and its tributaries. More than 1,000 campsites exist at Lake Mead. (Note: Hikers are warned to carry enough water, as the springwater is no longer deemed safe for drinking.) Another dam is that at Glen Canyon, 710 feet high, which impounds 186-mile-long Lake Powell in Arizona and Utah. The Glen Canyon Bridge, 1,271 feet long and 700 feet high, is one of the world's highest and longest. This particular dam galvanized intense and legitimate opposition from the conservation and environmental groups, but most Americans still delight in what they have built, invented, and discovered. If they haven't built or discovered it, they will invent it. So the tourism business is booming! Pleasure boats dot the dammed, or damned, waterways. Rafting is popular on rushing rivers.

Mobile homes form huge recreational encampments. Lodges and motels are springing up along the major thoroughfares. The Navajo and the Hopi have even constructed their own tourist facilities. Small airplanes and helicopters convey sightseers over the Grand Canyon, their motors breaking the peace of the canyon. Hikers crowd the Kaibab Trail through the somber walls of Archean rocks of the Granite Gorge to the Colorado River which the Havasupai Indians call the Place of the Roaring Sound. Great gashes have been made by open-pit coal mines, huge thermoelectric power plants have been constructed, oil and gas resources are being exploited, uranium mining has undergone a boom and bust. And now there are real problems! Let us explain.

Congress established the General Land Office in 1812 to give away the public domain. After time, there were 349 land offices in thirty-one states. "Doing a land-office business" was an expression derived from those times. The Grazing Service managed rangelands, but it became controversial by wanting to increase grazing fees. So the Bureau of Land Management (BLM) was formed in 1946 to supplant the General Land Office and the

Grazing Service. The BLM now manages 342 million acres (534,375 square miles) of public land. This is an enormous area, approximately equivalent to the aggregate area of Arizona, Colorado, Nevada, New Mexico, and Utah. The BLM lands are the residual land, the lands not taken by the homesteaders, the railroads, and the military. They are the rejected lands, but what lands they are! They embrace about a third of the nation's coal reserves, huge oil and gas reserves, 80 percent of the nation's high-grade oil shale, and a third of the known uranium deposits. Moreover, 20,000 ranchers have grazing permits for sheep and cattle on the public domain. But bear in mind enlightened dietary concerns and that only 4 percent of America's beef comes from cattle grazed on these public lands.

The San Juan Basin is in the eastern part (the Navajo Section) of the Colorado Plateau. It is the Four Corners Area, which we shall traverse on our route from Durango, Colorado, to Kayenta, Arizona. This basin has 26,000 square miles (equivalent to the size of South Carolina or West Virginia), mostly BLM and Navajo reservation land. It is one of the richest paleontological and archeological areas of the world, and with two billion tons of coal! Within this basin is Chaco Culture National Historical Park, site of thirteen major world-famous ruins, including Pueblo Bonito, and hundreds of smaller ones that represent culmination of pre-Columbian Pueblo civilization. This is a serene area, now menaced by ugly nets of power lines, and by strip-miners whose activities accelerate erosion and produce blasting noise and heavy truck and rail traffic. Skeptics from afar should visit the havoc wrought upon the land between Gallup, New Mexico, and Window Rock, Arizona. The land has been breached by ugly open scars, but more tragic is the deep division wrought upon the Navajo nation by those Indians who want quick money at the price of environmental degradation and social dislocation. Gallup, the Indian capital of the United States, now is the number-one center in the Southwest (some say in the entire U.S.) for Saturday night alcoholism. The coal is consumed in thermo-electric plants which now cast a pall of smoke over the Grand Canyon. Grants, New Mexico, has gone through a uranium boom and bust cycle. Real estate there is currently priced at only cents on the dollar, an ideal spot for inflation-ridden retirees seeking refuge from dependence on TV dinners. The population surge in the Sun Belt areas of California and southern Arizona is making new demands on water as well as on power. Re-read those glorious descriptions in the Great Surveys and revel once again at the landscape paintings of Thomas Moran, for the West is rapidly changing.

The Colorado Plateau region, however, still retains much wide-open land, untrammeled, and with vast vistas of ethereal beauty that inspire the spirit. Travel can be ever so pleasant. It is hoped that it can give us all a long-range perspective.

PART TWO

The Itinerary

Beyond the Great Divide

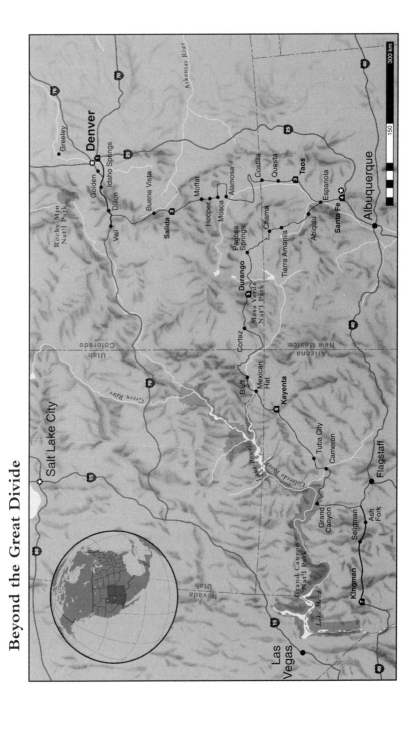

BEYOND THE GREAT DIVIDE

Ordinary travel guides, especially in the United States, emphasize the exceptional or unusual features of an area. Americans love to brag about their biggest, broadest, newest, oldest, longest, or tallest. This is an apparently incurable aberration known to professional diagnosticians as megalomania. Nevertheless, this aspect of travel is fun though obviously absurd after having seen the tallest monument in five different places, the world's longest tunnel in four different states, and the globe's highest windmill in seventeen locations. The situation in the land "beyond the Great Divide," however, has many genuinely superlative aspects. We can exclaim and yet deal here with reality. It is indeed a grand land! As we proceed we will marvel at the vast vistas, sense the emotions of early explorers, recapture the thrills of past adventurers, feel the urge of those concerned citizens who seek to preserve and conserve, perceive the push of the stalwart to conquer, or just surge forth to capture the next grand horizon.

Our tour "Beyond the Great Divide" takes us to exceptional places; that is no exaggeration. There is, for example, no other cut in the Earth's crust so geologically revealing nor so chromatically transcendent as the Grand Canyon in Arizona. That is not all; the rest is to discover—to discover not just the superlatives, but also the common denominators that deepen our understanding of this part of the American West, enhance our appreciation for its diverse lands and people, and anticipate its tomorrow. So let us start our grand sojourn from the heart of Denver, "Gateway to the West."

Denver, Colorado, to Salida, Colorado

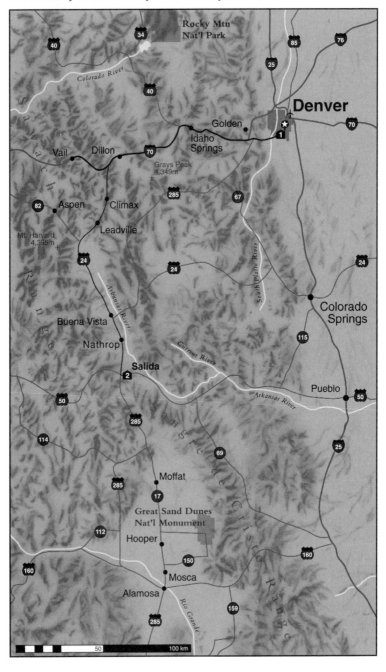

△ Day One

DENVER, COLORADO, TO SALIDA, COLORADO, 208 MILES

The first day's route is from the State Capitol, 10 miles straight west on Colfax Avenue, onto regular I-70, over the foothill zone and up the Rocky Mountain rampart, through the old gold-mining center of Idaho Springs, onward by other famed former mining districts, past mountain peaks exceeding 14,000 feet elevation, through the long Eisenhower Memorial Tunnel, to the renowned international ski resort of Vail, east and then south to the world's great molybdenum mine at Climax (11,320 feet), to the fabled town of Leadville, thence southward along the Arkansas Valley to the mountain-embraced town of Salida (7,050 feet).

Denver, Colorado, to Idaho Springs, Colorado, 25 miles, I-70

The *Civic Center* of *Denver* is at the intersection of north-south-trending Broadway Drive and the east-west-aligned Colfax Avenue. The Civic Center is an attractive, formally landscaped area with several structures grouped around it, including the State Capitol, the U.S. Mint, the Denver Public Library, the Municipal Building, the Greek Theater, the Pioneer Monument, the Denver Art Museum, and the Colorado History Museum. Dominating the Civic Center, at the eastern edge, is the *State Capitol,* a neoclassic-style granite structure with a gold-plated dome and Corinthian

Skyscrapers in Denver's central business district. Photograph by Cotton Mather.

porticoes fronting each of the four entrances. To the west and across the Civic Center from the State Capitol is the four-story Municipal Building, an impressive granite edifice with concave facade of Doric columns and a large central portico. Enhancing the Civic Center are the Pioneer Monument on the north side and the Greek Theater on the south side. This Civic Center is one of the West's most impressive public arenas; it was particularly striking until recent decades when the skyscrapers of the adjacent central business district became visually overwhelming. (An excellent historical appraisal of the Civic Center can be found in William H. Wilson's award-winning book, *The City Beautiful Movement,* published in 1989.)

We proceed westward from the State Capitol for 10 miles on Colfax Avenue, Business I-70, and then join regular I-70. Much of the early development on Colfax Avenue (west of the South Platte River and Federal Boulevard) was by Jewish people who established shops, kosher restaurants, newspapers, and movie houses. They also founded in 1899 the first nonsectarian hospital for tubercular patients. Denver was heralded in the early 1900s as an ideal place for tubercular patients, especially if they slept on open porches at all seasons to breathe in fresh air. Small wonder that Denver now has few of those tubercular patients still living! Its air is now among the worst in the western United States, along with Los Angeles, Phoenix, Boise, and Salt Lake City.

The first 8 miles west of the State Capitol represent largely the older U.S. highway model leading through an American city. It is a rather typical urban auto-strip with fast-food businesses, auto-service stations, drugstores, cleaners, two large shopping complexes, and a few older motels. The new urban highway model is the urban by-pass highway, represented by I-70 to the north of downtown Denver and along which are the newest motels and restaurants built to serve the trans-America tourists and truck drivers.

Immediately after joining I-70, we start through the "hogback" zone, or the mountain foothills. At 2.5 miles after joining regular I-70, note on the left the highly inclined sedimentary strata in the hogback. A hogback is formed when uptilted sedimentary rock is inclined to such a degree that the dip-slope of the rock and the escarpment face produce a nearly symmetrical ridge profile. These hogback sedimentary strata are the nearly horizontal rock strata of the Great Plains that have been severely uptilted along the face of the Rocky Mountain Front. West of the hogback zone we shall increase our altitude and proceed into a zone of older (Precambrian) crystalline rocks.

Five miles after joining I-70 (at exit 256), note fancy highland homes on both sides of the highway. The foothills here are mostly grass-covered at lower elevations. Higher elevations have much pine and some juniper. The most expensive housing has controlled access at an entrance gate. Most houses are separate residences, but some condominiums and a few office buildings have been constructed near some highway exits. Residential development here originally was for persons commuting to employment in Denver. Now some office building is being initiated to eliminate commuting for persons dwelling in the suburban zone.

Idaho Springs, Colorado, to Vail, Colorado, 77 miles, I-70

Fifteen miles after joining I-70, we leave the highland home zone and enter a narrow gorge with a small stream. Four miles farther, we pass through a short tunnel. Slightly more than 1 mile beyond, take the *Idaho Springs* business route. Then 0.7 mile farther, stop on the right; a good space is available there for parking and taking a photograph of the *Argo Gold Mill.*

There are self-guiding tours here and a mining museum. Central City is 8 miles northwest of the Argo Gold Mill here in Idaho Springs. The mining district of Central City-Idaho Springs has yielded nearly $200 million worth of gold, silver, lead, zinc, tungsten, and copper. Mining started in 1859 and soon mines appeared on most of the slopes. Idaho Springs also won fame in the 1860s as a spa with mineral springs having curative value.

Proceed from the Argo Gold Mill on the angle street to the left through the old business street of Idaho Springs with its brick and stone structures of the late 1800s. In the business district is an old locomotive with coal tender and passenger coach from the early mining period. The main business today in Idaho Springs is tourism. At the end of the business district, turn left and resume travel on I-70 West. Note 1.2 miles farther on the left the ruins of the *Old Stanley Mines.* You are now in the Colorado Mining Belt which was the main mining zone in Colorado from 1860 until 1885. About 5.8 miles beyond the Old Stanley Mines on the right (at exit 232, egress to Empire and Granby) are "mobile" homes for skiers. In another 4 miles on the left (at exit 228 into Georgetown) are ski condominiums. Take this exit into *Georgetown* (8,640 feet) and proceed 0.8 mile and park before the sign (marked "Old Town Business District") next to the picnic tables. Bus traffic cannot drive through the Historic Business District; it is too narrow. You will enjoy a 30-minute stroll west (ahead) and to the left through this living museum and thence back to your vehicle.

After resuming travel, you will reenter I-70; note the road gates that can be closed when winter driving conditions warrant this for your safety. Glaciated terrain becomes evident above 8,000 feet elevation with terminal morraines and U-shaped valleys. Two miles farther along, you will arrive at *Silver Plume* (9,175 feet), a silver-mining town which ceased most mining operations by 1900. This town has had a population explosion in relative terms, having increased about 21 percent in the past two decades: current population is 152 persons. Ten miles beyond the suburban fringe of Silver Plume, you will observe ski slopes and a ski lift on the left. Just beyond these ski slopes, you will enter the 1.7-mile-long *Eisenhower Memorial Tunnel* (11,013 feet). This tunnel, completed in 1973, goes under *Loveland Pass* (11,922 feet) and was named after President Dwight David Eisenhower (b. 1890; d. 1969), who conceived of the interstate highway system for the United States. Loveland Pass was not used as a highway until 1931; one can still use this route, however, by following old U.S. Highway 6, which branches off I-70 to the south and then rejoins I-70 at Dillon, 18 miles to the west.

Ten miles beyond Eisenhower Memorial Tunnel is a fine scenic overlook (9,150 feet). That 10 miles is a continuous highway downslope of 6 to 7 percent grade. The view south from the overlook is of *Bald Mountain* (13,681 feet) and *Mount Guyot* (13,370 feet). Arnold Guyot (b. 1807; d. 1884) was a Swiss-American geographer and lifelong friend of the world-famous glaciologist Louis Agassiz (b. 1807; d. 1873). Guyot was a professor at Princeton University in New Jersey from 1854 until his death. At Agassiz's suggestion, Guyot in 1838 initiated his studies of glaciers. His studies on alpine glaciers remain classic scientific investigations, for example his *Earth and Man, Lectures on Comparative Physical Geography in Its Relation to the History of Mankind* (translated by Professor C. C. Felton, 1949). To the southeast from this scenic overlook is *Torrey's Peak* (14,267 feet) and *Gray's Peak* (14,270 feet). *Lake Dillon,* in the foreground, stores water for the city of Denver. This water is tunneled 23 miles under the Continental Divide. To the southeast you are viewing the Continental Divide; waters to the west drain to the Pacific Ocean and waters to the east drain to the Atlantic Ocean. The town just west of Lake Dillon is *Frisco*, a mining camp during the 1870s.

Silverthorne (8,790 feet) and *Dillon,* 12 miles west of the Eisenhower Memorial Tunnel, comprise a complex of big motels and thousands of condominiums for ski patrons.

Twenty-four miles beyond the Eisenhower Memorial Tunnel is *Vail Pass* (10,662 feet). Past this pass is another long descent with mostly 6 to 7 percent grades. Although we are on a superhighway, trucks with over 30,000 pounds gross weight have a legal speed limit of 30 miles per hour. Note numerous truck runaway ramps.

Leave I-70 at exit 176 into *Vail*. This is 13.4 miles beyond Vail Pass. Just before this exit, on the left, is one of the United States's longest and narrowest golf courses—a consequence of its crowded location in a narrow mountain valley.

You are not permitted to drive through Vail. From exit 176, follow signs to the parking ramp for buses and cars. After parking, you may take the town's buses or walk. The bus stops at the lower level of the parking ramp.

Vail is linked to the Denver airport by regular ground transportation, and America West Airlines provides service from Phoenix and from Los Angeles (telephone 800-247-5692) as of this writing.

Vail is the United States's premier ski resort. It was established in 1962 and in 1989 it hosted the World Alpine Ski Championships. The sister resort, *Beaver Creek,* 10 miles to the west, includes residences of numerous celebrities, including that of former President Gerald Ford and his wife, Betty.

A Bavarian motif pervades Vail, and it has evolved from a winter to a year-round resort. The town has about seventy restaurants; some of them are indeed elegant. And there are numerous fine lodges as well as a few that emphasize the economy theme.

Vail Valley affords a great range of recreational activities, including skiing, ice-skating, tennis, horseback riding, hiking, sleigh riding, riding the chairlifts, nearby river floating, mountain lake and trout stream fishing, and golfing on four eighteen-hole public courses and on one private course (open mid-May to mid- October).

In addition, the town has indoor swimming pools, the Vail Nature Center, and a very attractive library. Vail hosts a special event every weekend, winter and summer. From July to September, the Vail Institute sponsors musical and cultural programs. Vail is high (8,150 feet) in the Rockies, tops as a ski resort, and attractive at all seasons.

Vail, Colorado, to Climax, Colorado, Molybdenum Mine, 37 miles, Highway 91

Our next objective is to visit the world's major molybdenum mine, the *Climax Mine,* at *Fremont Pass.* Return east on I-70 for 20 miles, and then go southward for 12 miles on State Highway 91 to the pass, which is about at the tree line and the zone of alpine tundra. Snow does fall in the pass in every month of the year; the average annual snowfall is about 300 inches (25 feet). Winter temperatures are severe, frequently falling to minus 30 degrees Fahrenheit.

The saga of the Climax Mine began in 1879 when Sergeant Charles J. Senter, recently retired from the Indian wars, discovered molybdenum ore at his gold claim at 12,000 feet on Bartlett Mountain, which overlooks Fremont Pass. Molybdenum had been identified first (i.e., recognized as a distinct element) in 1778 by Karl W. Scheele (b. 1742; d. 1786), a Swedish chemist. The word "molybdenum" is derived from the Greek *molybdos,* which means "lead-like." The discovery did not make Senter rich: in 1900, he was still a hardrock prospector, subsisting by washing gold out of the gravels near his little cabin close to Fremont Pass.

Scientists at the Colorado School of Mines (established in 1874 in Golden), in 1901, identified the Bartlett Mountain mineral as molybdenumite, and soon others were staking claims near Senter's. By 1916, the American Metals Company, a subsidiary of the German corporation Metalgesellschaft, had consolidated numerous claims and had established the Climax Molybdenum Company. Climax was the name of the station house, at Fremont Pass, of the Denver and South Park Railroad. Soon there were small crushers and mills plus facilities for the 300 employees, many of whom were Spanish-Americans and Mexicans.

The mine's gray metal began coming into modest demand before World War I as an alloy—in light-bulb filaments, for instance—but it was not until the 1920s that a young chemical engineer for the Climax Company, Brainerd F. Phillipson, induced Eastern steel manufacturers to use molybdenum in considerable quantities to produce harder steel alloys (i.e., to strengthen and harden steel).

The Climax Molybdenum mining operation was being done on a massive scale. The ore body was immense, but of very low grade. Research, however, during World War I brought revolutionary changes in mining technology, among them more powerful explosives, improved drills, and electric power. Mining by the Climax Molybdenum Company was rapidly expanding with the growth in demand from the large U.S. corporations. Climax sold the then-amazing total of 718,000 pounds of molybdenum from Bartlett Mountain in 1925.

The mining operations initially were underground where working conditions were dangerous and arduous. Numerous lives were lost. Work at this altitude, also, had side effects of *soroche,* or "mountain sickness." Workers complained of headaches, nausea, and dizziness, and soon quit. The company had one of the highest labor turnovers in U.S. industry.

Enormous changes occurred after 1927. The company undertook in 1928 the organization of a company town. The company's first year of profit was in 1929, and the following decade was one of great development. By 1939, the company was the world's chief source of molybdenum, employed over 1,000 men, and had virtually eliminated the fatal accident rate. The company town, with the highest post office in the nation, had 175 modern houses of four to nine rooms each, plus a variety of recreational facilities. But by 1960, the company town was being closed to make room for mill expansion. (By 1965, 60 million pounds of molybdenum from the mine were being used each year, most of it in steel production.) Most of the workers were now living in *Leadville,* and commuting from there. The employment roll soon reached 2,000.

Fall season at the huge Climax, Colorado, molybdenum mill in Fremont Pass at 11,300 feet elevation. Photograph by Cotton Mather.

Open-pit mining was initiated in the 1940s. This entailed the use of huge pieces of equipment, including electric shovels, bulldozers, and immense trucks. By 1980, the individual miner was removing 500 times as much ore as his counterpart of 1880. And over half of Colorado's total 1980 metal production of $600 million came from just the Leadville-Climax locale. Gaping holes and tailings disposal of the open pit operations became public issues. Environmentalists were now pitted against pit mining. Complete restoration of the original contours (to the extent possible) and seeding native grasses have been included in the company's program and safeguards have been established pertaining to water quality. The tailings pond, however, cannot be restored until the mining is completed. In the meantime, blotches on the landscape are highly visible and completely exposed alongside Colorado Highway 91.

The 1980s brought a shock to mining in the Leadville-Climax area. Prices and demand for molybdenum crashed, laborers were laid off, production was suspended, and the Japanese developed synthetic compound substitutes. Most world mining booms are succeeded by a bust, and it is unclear when economic conditions might improve for mining in this area.

Leadville, Colorado, to Granite, Colorado, 17 miles, Highways 91 and 24

Leadville (10,188 feet) is 12 miles ahead, more than 3,000 feet down from the Continental Divide at Fremont Pass and into the Arkansas River drainage system.

The *Arkansas Valley* is the northern part of the *Rio Grande Rift*. This rift, or structural valley, is faulted (or displaced along fractures on both edges) and continues southward through the *San Luis Valley* and onward into New Mexico where it is occupied by the Rio Grande. We follow this rift valley to *Salida* and thence southward into New Mexico.

Trending north-south, to the east, is the *Mosquito Range*. Also trending north-south, but to the west, is the *Sawatch Range*. These ranges are the flanks here of the down-faulted anticline or rift. The sedimentary rocks of the Mosquito Range are dipping to the east. The sedimentary rocks of the Sawatch Range are dipping to the west. The peaks of the Sawatch Range are mainly Precambrian (very old) gneiss and schist. Granite underlies the rift, but is at the surface near the town of *Granite,* located in the rift valley, about 15 miles south of Leadville. Great gravel terraces line both sides of the Arkansas Valley. They merge upvalley with glacial morraines. Leadville is on these terraces.

Leadville is the prototype of boom-and-bust mining towns in the Southern Rockies. Gold mining in Colorado started in 1858 with placer deposits in the Denver area. The next year gold strikes were made to the west in the mountains. Shortly thereafter, numerous mining camps appeared throughout much of the Southern Rockies. Towns such as *Cripple Creek, Silverton,* and *Aspen* sprang forth almost overnight. Gold was discovered in *California Gulch,* in the Leadville district, in 1860. Within four months, more than 5,000 miners were working that gulch. Two years later, the placer deposits had been almost exhausted. The place was nearly deserted and it was busted. But by 1880, Leadville was deep into silver mining and had a population of about 40,000. Horace A. W. Tabor (b. 1830; d. 1899), known as Silver Dollar Tabor, was one of the few who had remained from the gold-mining phase.

From the Matchless Mine at Leadville, he took silver worth $10 million. He was, suddenly, fabulously wealthy. He became lieutenant governor of Colorado, made generous donations, built opera houses, divorced his wife, and married young and beautiful Elizabeth McCourt ("Baby") Doe (b. 1862; d. 1935). Leadville really boomed. Construction spurted. Mercantile operators profiteered. Mining-stock manipulation was reckless. Liquor flowed. Churches were constructed. Brothels were very busy. It may not have been paradise, but it was certainly a boisterous success while it lasted. There is a sad ending to the Tabor story. Horace Tabor eventually lost most of his fortune through his extravagances, and at his death begged his wife, Elizabeth, to hold the Matchless Mine, which he believed would yield wealth again. She was found frozen to death in a shack at the mouth of the mine, or so the story goes, where apparently she had lived alone for many years.

More than $11 million worth of silver was mined in 1880, and the Leadville district had a dozen smelters (heavy air polluters) and ore-reduction plants. But soon silver prices plunged, and there was the panic of 1893. Later, in that same decade, a minor revival of gold mining occurred. Lead, zinc, and manganese mining was active in the first two decades of the 1900s and whisky distilling in the deserted mine shafts contributed to the economy and the consternation of the Woman's Christian Temperance Union (WCTU); this was during the Prohibition Era (1919 to 1933), when the sale of alcoholic beverages was prohibited by an amendment to the U.S. Constitution. As mining at the Leadville locale was finally ending, molybdenum mining at Climax was developing. Leadville then housed some of the molybdenum miners. But now the real support of Leadville is tourism.

Leadville is marketing its colorful past. The town has eight museums, the Tabor Opera House, the Silver Dollar Saloon, tours of the Matchless Mine, and narrated train trips on the Leadville, Colorado and Southern Railway to Climax; the two-and-one-half-hour trips are run from May 27 to September 4. The town of Leadville has some overnight accommodations, including bed-and-breakfasts (B&Bs). However, the facilities are mostly modest and limited in number. Consequently, in the summer tourist season, most people seek lodging elsewhere. Restaurants that feature mining town grub are available. Colorado's old mining towns have a rather tawdry aspect that reflects their heritage, but these old mining towns are bustling meccas in summer and in the fall when the foliage is brilliant.

The 4-mile stretch of U.S. Highway 24 leading southwest of Leadville goes past great slag heaps and the ruins of former mining ventures. The Arkansas Valley Smelter, built in 1877, produced these slag heaps. Two miles farther was *Malta,* no longer shown on road maps, which once had a charcoal-burning industry for the Leadville smelters. You can just imagine the extent of the pollution in those days.

The *Arkansas River* follows the rift, or structural, valley between Leadville and Granite—a distance of 17 miles. The valley here is paralleled on the east and the west by mountains that rise above the tree line (about 11,500 feet). The valley is referred to as a "park"; that is, a treeless valley or basin in the mountains. Between the treeless valley and the treeless mountain heights is a coniferous mid-altitude zone. Most of the valley is used for ranching, although you will observe some fishing and hunting cabins. This is big game country. Have you bagged an elk today?

Granite is a hamlet with one store that sells gas, groceries, fishing tackle, bait, and liquor—all necessities for sport enthusiasts! Next to the store is the Country Peddler Restaurant which serves high cuisine, at 8,946 feet. This food consists of such delectables as biscuits with gravy, char-broiled hamburgers, and homemade pies. The Arkansas River divides the hamlet. U.S.

A 1948 fall scene of a famous Middlewestern cattle buyer (right) and a rancher at a ranch in the Arkansas River valley in Colorado. Log barns and board fences are still common. Photograph by Cotton Mather.

Highway 24 and the business establishments are on the west side of the river. East of the river are houses, fishing cabins, and the railway. A one-lane bridge (15-ton capacity) spans the stream. (Hunters should exert caution when overloaded with liquor.)

Just south of Granite, note the old stagecoach road on the east side of the river.

At 17 to 22 miles beyond Granite, the Arkansas River is in a gorge. The stream gradient increases markedly.

At 26 miles beyond Granite, on the left is a large cluster of "mobile" homes used by fishermen. *Mount Harvard* (14,420 feet) is on the right horizon. Beyond, also on the right, is *Mount Yale* (14,196 feet). Many roadside signs advertise pack trips, trail rides, camping sites, and home sites along the Arkansas River. This is principally beef-ranching territory, but with many horses for the dudes.

Buena Vista, Colorado, to Salida, Colorado, 26 miles, Highways 24 and 291

Buena Vista (7,954 feet) is about midway in the 61 miles between Leadville and Salida, and it is the main town (population 2,000) between Leadville and Salida. Buena Vista was founded in 1879

A cow herd is moved from government-owned highland pastures to privately-owned valley land where they will be wintered. Photograph by Cotton Mather.

by silver prospectors, and two years later had a smelter. Today, it is almost exclusively a tourist town with several motels, gas stations, restaurants, campgrounds, rafting stations, liquor dispensaries, bed-and-breakfasts, gift shops, grocery stores, coin-operated laundries, and offices of realtors anxious to make a sale.

Beyond Buena Vista, 1.7 miles on the left, is a prison. On the right is *Mount Princeton* (14,197 feet), another peak in the "Collegiate Range."

Nathrop, 7.8 miles south of Buena Vista, with a purported population of fifty-six souls, offers recreational supplies, rafting excursions, a taxidermy, liquor, and a church for restoration of the soul.

The Arkansas Valley, from Buena Vista to Salida, broadens considerably. This section has large irrigated hayfields. Beef-cattle herds graze, under government permit, in summer on the alpine pastures. These cattle—mostly Angus, Hereford, and crossbred animals—are moved onto the valley pastures and hayfields in the fall season and are wintered there on hay and protein supplement. They seem content in such a beautiful landscape as this, so content, in fact, that even the wary taxpayer, who is paying for much of the irrigation in the West, can muster a smile.

Salida, Colorado, to Taos, New Mexico

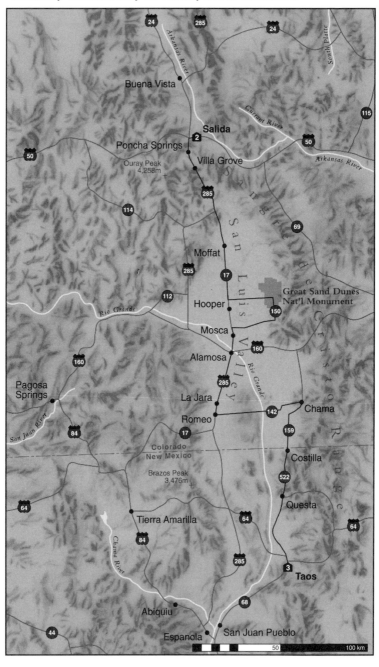

△ Day Two

SALIDA, COLORADO, TO TAOS, NEW MEXICO, 234 MILES

The second day's route is from Salida, south over Poncha Pass, through the San Luis Valley—the largest and most diverse of the "parks" in the Southern Rockies. In the San Luis Valley, we shall visit the Great Sand Dunes National Monument, ranching and irrigated farming areas, the old Spanish-American towns of San Acacio and San Luis; and proceed to Taos with its famous Indian pueblo, Spanish-American community, and Anglo-American art colony.

Salida, Colorado, to Moffat, Colorado, 44 miles, Highways 50, 285, and 17

Salida (7,050 feet), the county seat of Chaffee County, has had a stable population of about 5,000 for the past five decades. The town was founded by the Denver and Rio Grande Railroad in 1880, and had an early history as a rail junction and smelting center. Laura Evans, a widely known if not universally respected madam, ran a brothel here from 1896 to 1950. Today, Salida is best known for its basin-like setting with magnificent 14,000-feet mountains around it. It is popular, also, for great fishing; contact the Division of Wildlife office in Salida for information (telephone 719-539-3529).

The Arkansas River near Salida, Colorado. Photograph by George F. Thompson.

Downtown Salida, Colorado. Photograph by George F. Thompson.

To the west of Salida, 21 miles, is the *Monarch Ski Area*, one of Colorado's best. About 50 miles east is the *Royal Gorge* where the Arkansas River roars through a narrow canyon between the Front Range and the Wet Mountains. This area is highly commercialized and littered with billboards. Yet it is a spectacular canyon with nearly vertical walls and is spanned by one of the world's highest suspension bridges, 1,000 feet above the river. Floating and rafting on the Arkansas River are very popular near Salida; contact Moondance River Expeditions in Salida for floating and rafting trips (telephone 719-539-2113).

Visit the business district of Salida. It is an architectural gem, a National Historic District, with a fine set of century-old buildings.

And take a plunge into Colorado's largest indoor hot-spring pool, built in 1937 as a WPA (Works Progress Administration) project, at 410 West Rainbow Boulevard in Salida. The hot mineral water is piped from several miles away. Cakes baked at these altitudes will not rise as they do at lower levels. Business in Salida, however, is little into cake baking. Rather, it is concerned primarily with ranch trade and tourism. It is one of Colorado's most serene towns and in a lovely setting. May it always remain so.

We travel west from Salida on U.S. 50 for 4 miles to *Poncha Springs*. On the right, near the eastern edge of town, are the Chaffee County fairgrounds. County agricultural fairs are a long-established American tradition, although their popularity has been waning in recent decades. Most county fairs feature competition with blue ribbon awards for fine household and farm exhibits. Added features are the 4-H youth programs and the displays of farm machinery and industrial wares. The fairgrounds usually include a racetrack for horses or car racing, amusement rides such as a Ferris wheel and carousel, and a bandstand for C-W (Country and Western) and other musical delights.

Poncha Springs is a highway crossroads with just a few buildings, including the structure for the fire department, a convenience store, a gas station, a small lumberyard, a gift shop, and the old Jackson Hotel (no longer in use). At Poncha Springs, turn southward onto U.S. 285 and onward then to *Poncha Pass* (9,010 feet). The highway has three lanes up to the summit to facilitate vehicular passing. This relatively low pass is the divide of the Rio Grande and the Arkansas River watersheds. A toll road was constructed over this pass in 1875. Now it is free and serves as the main northern entrance to the *San Luis Valley*. At the pass, the coniferous forest is patchy with extensive areas of mountain pasture. Cattle graze these government-owned pastures in summer, during which season the ranchers pack in salt blocks and check the condition of the cattle. The salt blocks are for the cattle and are scattered to encourage even more grazing. No doubt deer and elk like the salt, too.

Seven miles south of the pass, note on the left the extensive irrigated hay meadows. Hay is cut and baled in summer. By

South Park, Colorado: Range cattle in the fall season that summered on government land in the Saguache Mountains now chow down in this rich valley land. Photograph by Cotton Mather.

October, the high peaks are snow-capped and it is a great sight to see the huge cattle herds "cleaning up" the hay meadows. Hunters are out in full force and blaze orange gear (for safety) during the fall season. Many use "campers" on pickup trucks for living quarters and four-wheel vehicles to roam into rough terrain.

The hamlet of *Villa Grove* (7,952 feet) is 14 miles south of Poncha Pass. It is comprised of a dozen houses; a few mobile homes; Doc's auto and truck repair; three gas pumps; the Mount Valley Liquor Store; the Turquoise Rock and Mineral Shop; the Villa Grove Trade store with automotive, hunting, and fishing supplies, homemade pies, delicatessen sandwiches, and (that critical commodity) ice; Jim Woodward's wild game processing; and Kerber Creek Woodworks.

The junction of U.S. Highway 285 and State Highway 17 is 5 miles south of Villa Grove; follow State Highway 17 for 36 miles to the route leading east to *Great Sand Dunes National Monument,* which we visit after first seeing *Moffat* and *Hooper.* About 3 miles south on State Highway 17, on the right, is what you might surmise to be a frog pond. The billboard there, however, informs us that it is a private fishing lake on the Lazy KV Estates. These estates are one-acre lots for sale plus about two dozen "manufactured and mobile homes" and a Baptist church.

The northern San Luis Valley is excellent ranch country. Across this natural grassland, note the scattered clumps of trees. These clumps are at ranchsteads which are usually comprised of a one-story frame family residence, one or two mobile homes for cowhands, a few sheds for special livestock handling and machine storage, plus corrals and loading chutes. Most of the hay is baled and stacked in the open. Cattle are wintered outside with hay and protein supplement as feed. Most calves are born in spring.

For several miles just south of Poncha Pass, snow fences line the west side of the highway. As we proceed to lower elevations, however, precipitation decreases, snowfall is light, and the snow fences are absent.

Winters in the San Luis Valley are severely cold. On the basin floor, temperatures stay low for weeks at a time, with nighttime lows of 10 to 20 degrees below zero Fahrenheit. In the central part of the San Luis Valley, the snow is light in amount and fluffy; it blows away readily and the highways are normally clear. At times, though, the snow may be rather wet and then it packs on the highways and makes driving hazardous.

Livestock are fenced in with three or four strands of barbed wire fastened to steel posts set one or one and one-half rods apart. A rod is an English unit of measurement equal to sixteen and one-half feet in length; it is quite useful in calculating field area because an acre equals 160 square rods.

Electric power lines on poles branch off the main lines along highways and lead to individual ranchsteads. All telephone lines here are buried.

The size of ranches varies greatly. Some ranches have more than 100,000 acres and a few are from old Spanish land grants. Three of the largest ranches were purchased recently by Japanese, one of which has an airfield and a golf course. Many smaller ranches are part-time operations where either the husband or the wife has off-ranch employment. These smaller ranches have only two or three sections (1,280 or 1,920 acres) of deeded land. In addition to deeded land, of course, most ranches have permits for summer grazing on government land in the mountains. Cattle graze these mountain pastures from about April to September.

Where are the sheep? They are mostly in the southern part of the San Luis Valley, in the Hispanic and the Mormon communities.

Moffat is a small village 31.1 miles south of Poncha Pass, east of the highway. It has a twelve-grade consolidated school; that is, children are bused in from as far away as twenty miles.

Hooper, Colorado, to Alamosa, Colorado, 46 miles, Highways 185 and 150

Hooper (7,550 feet) is 17.4 miles south of Moffat. It was laid out on a quarter section (160 acres). It had sixty-eight registered voters in April of 1990. But times have changed! In 1940, there was a Chevrolet garage, three grocery stores, a hardware store, a functioning railway depot, and a big potato warehouse. The railway was narrow-gauge from Alamosa to Salida and was built about 100 years ago for hauling farm products, but it went "belly-up" about 1948. The town is still incorporated and has a six-member board. There is a restaurant, a gas station, and a post office on the highway. East of the highway is the school with six grades, seventy-seven students, and eight buses. Pupils in grades seven to twelve go seven miles south to *Mosca*. Some town business buildings are empty and ripe for restoration, but Hooper does have a laundromat, the Masons have their lodge, and women belong to Rebecca Lodge. In addition, there is the Baptist church with about sixty worshippers on Sunday. Paul Williams is the present mayor

Midday on the main street of Hooper, Colorado, in the San Luis Valley. Photograph by Cotton Mather.

and, thanks to him and the remaining citizens of Hooper, the town has a neat little park with a picnic table.

The rural environs of Hooper produce potatoes, lettuce, carrots, alfalfa, and "beer barley." These crops are irrigated by wells that are 80 to 90 feet deep. The farm population is decreasing as farm size is increasing. Most farmers shop at *Alamosa,* 20 miles away. It makes no difference around Hooper whether you are rural or urban at nightfall, since everyone has television.

Great Sand Dunes National Monument, Colorado

Six miles south of Hooper, turn left and go about 20 miles east to the attractive visitor center at the *Great Sand Dunes National*

Monument (elevation 8,000 feet at the dune base) where you can get information and take advantage of the good "rest stop" facilities. As you get out of your car, note the adjacent towering peaks (Crestone at 14,294 feet and Blanca at 14,345 feet) of the *Sangre de Cristo Range.*

The Sangre de Cristo Range has an extraordinarily steep western face, a fault zone with major movement in Miocene-Pliocene time. The eastern side of the range was uplifted by faulting and tilting of Paleozoic sedimentary rocks.

The dunes cover an area of 80 square miles and rise 750 feet above their base. The dune sands are derived from igneous rocks from the *San Juan Mountains,* which are approximately 50 miles southwest. Prevailing winds much of the year in the San Luis Valley are westerly. Most of the dunes have an axis trending northwest-southeast, with gentle windward and steep leeward slopes.

This area was established as a national monument by President Herbert Hoover in 1932. The visitor center is open daily from0800 to 1700 except for being closed during all winter federal holidays (telephone 719-378-2312). One should allocate two hours for walking the dunes plus viewing exhibits at the visitor center.

Proceed southward 23 miles on Colorado Highway 150 from the monument. Turn right on U.S. 160 and go west 14 miles to Alamosa.

Alamosa (7,544 feet) has a population of about one person per foot elevation above sea level. It is the main ranch and farm trade center in the San Luis Valley, and accommodates a large tourist trade in the summer and fall seasons. The town has several good restaurants and four comfortable motels. *Adams State College,* founded in 1921, has a pleasant campus with about 2,500 students and 121 faculty members. The *Rio Grande,* which flows through the eastern edge of town, varies in volume greatly during the year. It is fed mainly by melting snow in early summer from its headwaters in the San Juan Mountains.

The *San Luis Valley,* which is approximately 88 miles long north-south and with a maximum east-west width of about 40 miles, extends southward almost to the New Mexico-Colorado boundary. It is a structural basin between the San Juan Mountains on the west and the Sangre de Cristo (Blood of Christ) Range on the east. Grass covers most of the basin floor, although the driest areas have greasewood and sagebrush. Average annual precipitation on the basin floor is about 8 inches, half of which occurs in July, August, and September when evaporation is at a maximum. The average frost-free season is from about May 30 to September 25, only 118 days in length because of the 7,000-feet elevation of the basin floor. While the basin floor appears almost flat, there are piedmont alluvial fans which merge into a *bajada,* or compound piedmont alluvial plain, along the east and west margins of the basin. What is not perceptible to the eye is that the northern part of the San Luis Valley is a closed basin. The *Saguache River* and the *San Luis River* (really pathetic little streams) in the north are swallowed up by evaporation in this dry region, by downward percolation into the deep alluvial deposits (in places 12,000 feet deep), or by flowing into ephemeral lakes. The southern part of the San Luis Valley, however, is drained by the master stream the *Rio Grande.* The Rio Grande has carved a gorge into igneous rock as it drains away from the San Luis Valley into New Mexico.

A great resource of the San Luis Valley is its artesian water. Impervious layers of clay and shale cap this underground water except where layers have been pierced by wells. There are several thousand flowing wells now in the valley! Most of the agriculture is in the southern half of the valley, through which we shall travel as we leave Alamosa.

La Jara, Colorado, to San Acacio, Colorado, 49 miles, Highways 285 and 142

La Jara (The Arrow) is 14 miles south on U.S. Highway 285 from Alamosa. Most of the agriculture in this sector is a combination of farming and ranching. The chief crops are potatoes, barley, and alfala. See the marked change in fencing from linear (for cattle) to woven (for sheep) wire; sheep are important in this area as well as are cattle. Not all the land is cropped; some is in natural range.

In La Jara (7,602 feet), note the grain elevator. Barley for malting is important in this area. At the south end of town, on the right, is the Roman Catholic church, with many Hispanic adherents. Ahead, on the left, is the Church of Jesus Christ of Latter Day Saints (Mormon), with Anglo adherents. Nearby are the railside facilities of the La Jara Potato Growers Association. Most potatoes here are marketed in the fall. Just beyond is a wool warehouse.

Three miles farther are three abandoned buildings along the highway and a barley elevator by the railway. This is the old town of *Bountiful,* a town with a beautiful name but with a present population of zilch.

At 21.3 miles south of Alamosa, at the moribund village of *Romeo,* turn left off U.S. Highway 285 onto State Highway 142. Follow 142 for 35 miles to *San Luis.*

Manassa, 3 miles east of Romeo, has seen better days. The old movie theater is closed. Two small businesses rent nocturnal Manassa escapes, here termed "videos." Only one building in town is large, new, and well-maintained: the large and impressive sanctuary and attached social hall of the Church of Jesus Christ of Latter Day Saints (LDS). A block east is the small Roman Catholic church. All the streets in this town are broad and the lots are large, laid out in Mormon style. Since pioneer days in the American West, the Mormons have been great urban designers and irrigation engineers. Manassa's claim to fame is that Jack Dempsey ("the Manassa Mauler"), the world's heavyweight boxing champion from 1919 to 1926, was born here in 1895. Dempsey apparently perceived Manassa's future and left town at an early age. He worked in mines and on railroads and later as a professional fighter in mining camps before gaining international fame.

Our road passes between two lava-capped hills, 6 miles east of Manassa. The one to the north is 1,300 feet higher than the highway, and the one to the south is 1,700 feet higher. Four miles farther, we cross the *Rio Grande* (Big River), which downstream for 1,000 miles forms the international boundary of the United States and Mexico. The Mexicans refer to the Rio Grande as "Río Bravo del Norte," or "Wild/Ferocious River of the North." As we cross the Rio Grande on this section, note the exposed basaltic lava. The San Luis Valley is bounded on the south by a lava plateau.

The heart of *San Acacio* (7,737 feet) is 11.2 miles beyond the Rio Grande. The Southern San Luis Valley Railway was constructed in 1910 from *Blanca,* 16 miles north of San Acacio, southward through San Acacio. This railway connected at Blanca with the Denver and Rio Grande Western Railroad. Many Hispanics farmed around San Acacio until the onset of a water shortage in the 1950s. Then the railway was abandoned, the fields fell into disuse, and by 1990 most of the farmhouses had disappeared. Today, little business remains in San Acacio. The population of San Acacio on 4 July 1991, including seven persons celebrating Independence Day in Alamosa, had dwindled to ninety-four persons. Surprisingly, the railway station is now being restored lovingly by a young couple from Fresno, California. Sporadically, they operate a restaurant in this station.

San Luis, Colorado, to Taos, New Mexico, 50 miles, Highways 159 and 522

The National Historic District of the Hispanic town of *San Luis* (7,586 feet) is 8.3 miles east of San Acacio. This town was founded by six Spanish families in 1851 who built adobe houses around a plaza with the outer walls of houses forming a wall as protection against the bellicose Ute Indians. Historically, San Luis has been a poor town, and this aspect has been well preserved. Note the empty commercial buildings on main street, although an attempt is being made to lure tourists by having some curio shops. Yet the town itself is a curio! This town has no franchised food establishments, but, fortunately, it does have some good Mexican cooking. On arrival at San Luis, turn right on State Highway 159. Of real interest at the south end of town, on the left, is the 860-acre community pasture reserved as a town common. Such a common was an aspect of many medieval town plans in Spain, and the planning principle still applies: Buy a place in San Luis and you will have a pasture for your cow! (Think what a real estate agent back East could do with that information.) The irrigation ditch for this pasture was constructed in 1852, and it is the oldest continuously used ditch in Colorado. (Note: For those who are interested in learning more about the importance of an irrigation ditch in a Hispanic town such as this, the best account is *Mayordomo: Chronicle of an Acequia in Northern New Mexico,* by Stanley Crawford. The book was awarded the 1988 Western States Book Award for Creative Nonfiction.)

The Colorado-New Mexico state line is 7.5 miles south of San Luis. Colorado State Highway 159 changes here to New Mexico State Highway 522. Follow State Highway 522 into *Taos.*

South of the state line 1.4 miles is *Costilla,* a charming village often overlooked by the busy traveler. Take State Highway 196 east a short hop into the town proper. Costilla once had an amazing four plazas. Now it has the remnants of these plazas and only a fraction of its earlier population. But it is worth a glimpse and, indeed, its Hispanic charm far outshines the much touted San Luis. Then return to State Highway 522 and proceed southward toward Taos.

Questa (7,469 feet), 20 miles south of Costilla, was, until recent years, just a trade center for the local farming and ranching community. Six decades ago it had 1,000 people. Now the official figure is about 600. But this is deceptive because two recent aspects have enlivened Questa: good old molybdenum mining up the Red River canyon to the east of town; and skiing and recreational activity tributary to Questa in the Sangre de Cristo Mountains to the east, including the *Ski Rio Area,* the *Red River Ski Area,* and *Taos Ski Valley.* Also, but to the west, is the *Rio Grande Gorge National Recreational Site.* Questa has a few motels and restaurants, none notable, so most motorists proceed to Taos, which has fine facilities.

Arroyo Hondo ("Deep Ditch"), a village 14 miles south of Questa, is in a fertile valley just west of the Sangre de Cristo Mountains. Quite a few *moradas* (Penitente chapels) are in this and other rather isolated mountain communities of northern New Mexico. Los Hermanos Penitentes is a Roman Catholic cult that still survives; it adheres to a belief in atonement through flagellation and mock crucifixions. The cult is secretive and persists with some guarantees of constitutional freedom. Although the church has attempted to suppress the Penitentes, they remain as a religious folk-survival.

Hippies had two main cores in the United States in the 1960s. The urban core was in the San Francisco Bay area and the rural core was in the secluded mountains of northern New Mexico. Communes were established in this latter region which includes the Arroyo Hondo locale. Most of the communes had disappeared by 1980.

Seven miles beyond Arroyo Hondo, we are on the outskirts of *Taos,* on the *Taos Plateau,* near the base of the Sangre de Cristo Mountains. Seven miles to the west is the impressive *Rio Grande Gorge Bridge,* a steel and concrete structure approximately 650 feet above the river. Observation platforms and shaded picnic tables by the bridge afford panoramic views of the gorge, incised into the basaltic lava of the Taos Plateau, and of the distant Sangre de Cristo Mountains that, here, hover over Taos. (Also, note the distinctive Zia symbol on the bridge railings; this is the same symbol that appears on the New Mexico state flag.) The Taos Plateau has some large shield volcanoes and many cinder cones.

Our entry into Taos (7,000 feet) takes us into a complex of three settlements: *Don Fernando de Taos* (or Taos proper), *Pueblo de Taos,* and *Rancho de Taos.* The three settlements have essentially merged with a population of about 4,500. Taos is a fascinating town to stroll around (if you can find a parking place), especially at eventide, and a great place for an overnight stay. Longtime visitors, however, regretfully acknowledge that Taos is becoming more congested every year—with people and T-shirt and ski shops—the result of a booming tourist and skiing industry.

△ *Day Three*

TAOS, NEW MEXICO, TO SANTA FE, NEW MEXICO, 70 MILES

On the third day we visit the Taos Pueblo, stop at the architecturally renowned mission church in Ranchos de Taos, then proceed along the Rio Grande to Española and onward for lunch at Santa Fe—one of the five most distinctive cities in the United States. The afternoon agenda includes a visit to the Indian Pueblos of Santa Clara and San Ildefonso and to the Hispanic community of Chimayó, then a return to Santa Fe.

Taos, New Mexico

Taos is a small Hispanic town with an Indian Pueblo at its northern edge and the old Indian farming community of *Ranchos de Taos* at its southern fringe.

The heart of Taos is the plaza, formerly bare and treeless, now with a covered bandstand, shaded walkways, and benches. Surrounding the plaza are art galleries, boutiques, restaurants, and the famous *La Fonda* hotel with its D. H. Lawrence paintings and Indian arts and crafts. In pleasant weather, you may enjoy relaxing on a plaza bench or gambolling around the plaza and along the side streets. Traffic, however, is usually snarled around the plaza and parking is limited. So perhaps you should park your car in the municipal lot northwest of the plaza and enjoy strolling around town.

Taos, New Mexico, to Santa Fe, New Mexico

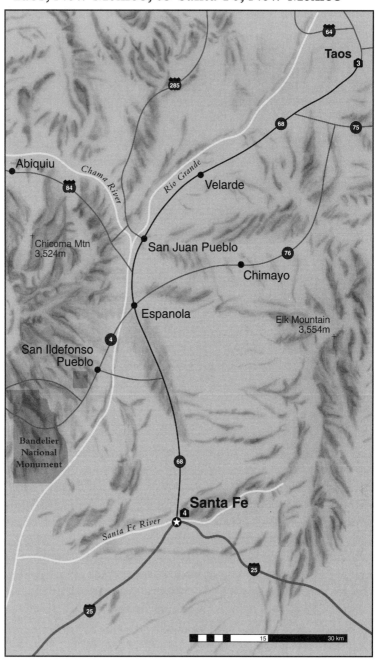

The resident population of Taos is about 60 percent Hispanic, 6 percent Indian, and the remainder mostly Anglo (Anglo, for the most part, means anyone who is not Indian or Hispanic). However, the non-resident tourist population is large and it is upon them that Taos is largely dependent.

Taos is an old town. It was known to European explorers from the time of Coronado (1540 to 1542), but was not settled by European stock until 1617. French traders appeared at the trading fairs in the eighteenth century, and the Americans arrived after 1820. Artists started coming about 1890, followed by writers. Famous people who have lived in Taos include painters Ernest L. Blumenschein (b. 1874; d. 1960) and Georgia O'Keeffe (b. 1887; d. 1986), writers Mable Dodge (b. 1879; d. 1962) and D. H. Lawrence (b. 1885; d. 1930), photographer Ansel Adams (b. 1902; d. 1984), and legendary frontiersman Kit Carson (b. 1809; d. 1868). Today, Taos is a major art center and the home of numerous writers, editors, potters, painters, weavers, musicians, jewelers, and antiquarians.

Taos had an incursion of hippies in the 1960s with negative community consequences, including strains on the local relief roll, eventual mendicancy, and considerable bitterness. Most of the hippies, however, have now disappeared or melted into the social mainstream.

Taos has a style of its own. It is a curious blend of five cultures: Hispanic, Indian, Anglo, the art world, and the ephemeral tourist. The individual types are all there on the plaza, on the side streets, and on the town fringe. Their community is a one-story sprawl of crooked streets with low adobe or pseudo-adobe residences, often sheltered behind adobe or wooden walls. One senses here a privacy lost to so much of the United States.

Taos, New Mexico, to Española, New Mexico, 46 miles, Highways 68 and 84/285

Taos Pueblo, two miles north of the plaza, has about 1,000 residents and an additional 1,000 members who live elsewhere. Their landholdings total about 95,000 acres. This Pueblo embodies the image most Americans have of the Indian Southwest. This image stems largely from two factors: its location adjacent to one of the nation's major art centers; and the spectacular multistoried, communal, adobe architecture of the dwellings, which have been endlessly photographed and painted and written about in books and magazine articles. The result has been terrific publicity and a lot of visitation. The site of Taos Pueblo has been occupied since the middle of the fourteenth century. The present mission church (listed on the National Register of Historic Places) actually sits upon the ruins of an earlier one destroyed in the Pueblo Revolt of 1680. Despite publicity to the contrary, Taos Pueblo is highly commercialized with many festivals open to the public and with a remarkable roster of charges for parking, photography, and touring. In addition, Indian vendors ply their wares in and adjacent to the Pueblo. While Taos and Cochiti drums are appreciated by collectors, the pottery of Taos and Picurís Pueblos is made of a micaceous material and can best be described as perhaps possessing a certain rustic appeal.

Our route out of Taos is via New Mexico Highway 68, which takes us along the Rio Grande to *Española,* and thence onward to Santa Fe. At the southern edge of Taos is *Ranchos de Taos* and the famous *Church of St. Francis of Assisi,* built in 1772. This adobe structure, with its two beautiful bell towers, is 120 feet long and has walls that are 4 feet thick. It is a wonderful edifice, elegant in its simplicity, and it merits at least a brief stop. Georgia O'Keeffe, in 1929 and 1930, made a number of now-famous paintings of this church, and those who are familiar with the work of photographer Paul Strand (b. 1890; d. 1976) will recall the hauntingly beautiful photographs he made of this church in 1931 and 1932.

The lava-walled gorge of the Rio Grande, south of Taos, New Mexico, is especially beautiful during the fall when the riverine cottonwood trees display their golden foliage. Photograph by Cotton Mather.

Our route southwestward along State Highway 68 from Ranchos de Taos (6,900 feet) descends 2,300 feet in 25 miles. Our descent is from the *Taos Plateau,* through which the Rio Grande flows briskly in a lava-walled gorge, to the valley of the Rio Grande near *Velarde.* A few flattish places along the river afford parking and picnicking areas or are large enough for an orchard or a tiny farm. This sector is very popular for river-rafting groups and canoeists.

Pilar ("Pillar"), 6.8 miles south of Ranchos de Taos, is a little community on a small delta. Before the Spanish came, it was a Jicarilla Apache settlement.

South of Pilar, near the junction of State Highways 68 and 75, in the locale referred to as *Embudo* ("Funnel")—a former Indian Pueblo—is the *Embudo Gauging Station.* The original gauging

SIDE TRIP TO PICURÍS PUEBLO

At a road junction 10 miles south of *Pilar,* a side trip that attracts some enlightened travelers is to go east on scenic State Highway 75 for approximately 17 miles to the small *Picurís Pueblo,* population about 250, whose landholdings total about 14,950 acres. The Pueblo is in a picturesque setting and has a small museum and cafe. Prehistoric ceremonial structures with wall paintings have been excavated here; the Pueblo was first occupied, according to archeologists, in the mid-thirteenth century. The Mission of San Lorenzo, with its white-faced church, was built about 1775; the original church was destroyed in the Pueblo Revolt of 1680 in which at least twenty Spanish soldiers were killed here. (For more information about this Pueblo, see "Picurís Pueblo," by Donald H. Brown, in *Handbook of North American Indians,* volume 9, Smithsonian Institution, Washington, D.C., 1979.)

Return west to State Highway 68 via 75.

station here was built by the famous geologist/explorer John Wesley Powell (b. 1834; d. 1902).

Seven miles beyond Embudo is *Velarde,* a community with apple and peach orchards and patches of famous New Mexico chiles. Roadside stands in the summer and autumn sell fruit and beautiful *ristras* (strings) of red chiles. The red chiles are popular for cooking (as are green chiles) and are often hung by house entrances as ornamentals. Tourists may discover that they can be purchased much more cheaply at *Hatch,* 283 miles to the south. Unless you like red-stained clothing, do not pack these succulent *ristras* in your suitcase!

The *San Juan Pueblo*, 10 miles south of Velarde and slightly west of our highway, has about 1,800 residents and 12,235 acres of landholdings. The headquarters of the *Eight Northern Pueblos* as well as a crafts cooperative is at San Juan. San Juan, under Spanish rule, was the capital of Nuevo Mexico from 1599 to 1609, whereupon the center of government was transferred to Santa Fe. The San Juan Mercantile and General Merchandise store was the oldest operating store in New Mexico until a few years ago when it was mysteriously destroyed by fire. Dr. Pijoan, a San Juan Indian and a distinguished doctor who practiced in one of the leading medical centers in the East, operated the San Juan Mercantile and Merchandise store after his retirement from medicine. Under his direction, this store was one of the foremost spots in the Southwest for obtaining fine Indian pottery. The six Pueblos of the Southwest that produce the finest pottery are Acoma, Hopi, San Ildefonso, San Juan, Santa Clara, and Zia Pueblos, though, of course, quality varies even among these. Dr. Pijoan displayed and merchandised the finest pottery from those Pueblos with the best interests of the Indians in mind as well as serving the tourists admirably. Today, his absence as a patron of ceramic art is deeply evident. The new crafts cooperative is an inadequate replacement.

Española (5,600 feet), just south of San Juan Pueblo, has a population of about 12,000. Española, at the junction of U.S. Highways 84 and 285 in addition to State Highways 30, 68, and 76, is a bustling blue-collar town. It is a striking example of what happens much too often in rapid U.S. growth when city leaders lack a environmental planning/design perspective, which leads to a chaotic mélange of fast-food joints, gas stations, liquor stores, and service establishments being plunked down apparently indiscriminantly along the thoroughfares. Seasoned travelers rush through Española and breathe a sigh of relief as they approach Santa Fe. Española, however, is experiencing rapid growth (twentyfold in the past five decades). Its location is central to most of the Indian Pueblos, to the old Spanish settlements of northern New Mexico, and to the centers of Taos, Santa Fe, and Los Alamos. Despite its centrality, most overnight tourists and persons sensitive to attractive amenities avoid Española. The blue-collar residents, however, appreciate the strips of nationally franchised businesses that emphasize fast service at minimum cost. Many of the residents commute daily to work at Los Alamos or Santa Fe. Española's blighted reputation among tourists is not enhanced by the local youth who often cruise menacingly in gangs of "lowrider" vehicles and by the clogged commuter traffic at rush hour.

Española, New Mexico, to Santa Fe, New Mexico, 24 miles, Highways 84/285

Ten miles south of Española, we pass *Pojoaque,* an ancient Tewa Pueblo. Subsequently, our route traverses colorful badlands and on the right is the sandstone formation, *Camel Rock.* We gradually ascend and the terrain is vegetated with dwarf piñon pine and juniper (also known as "p and j").

About 21 miles south of Española and 3.5 miles from the Santa Fe plaza are the grounds of the *Santa Fe Opera.* The Santa Fe Opera began in 1957 and won national acclaim through its director and founder, John Crosby. Performances are held from late June to the middle of August in a spectacular semi-open-air amphitheater which seats 1,765 persons. Tickets must usually be ordered long in advance, though "hawkers" usually have some for a premium price near the theater entrance. From the lowest priced seats, which are in the lofty back rows, one can see the star-studded sky and the distant lights of Los Alamos. In addition to such a view and the fine music is the display at intermission of the patrons' spectacular turquoise and silver jewelry. An experience long to remember!

As we enter the hilly north edge of Santa Fe, note to the left (east) the newer residential outskirts of the city. The homes are all Southwest in style, mainly of Santa Fe and Territorial architecture.

Santa Fe ("Holy Faith"), at 7,000 feet elevation, has an urban population of about 88,000. It is the state capital and is the oldest settlement in the U.S. West by people of European stock. Santa Fe was chosen as a Spanish provincial capital in 1609, and for nearly four centuries it has remained a seat of government, albeit under four different flags—Spain, Mexico, the Confederate States of

America, and the United States of America. The city in modern times has been off the track of main railway lines and has never developed a noteworthy industrial component. It has, however, become a nationally prominent center of the arts and has attracted affluent people. But its growth has lagged behind Albuquerque and Las Cruces. It is now only the third largest city in New Mexico, yet it is feeling the effects of clogged automobile traffic and limited parking along its picturesque but narrow, winding streets. And Santa Fe's cost of living is high and its real estate is expensive.

Santa Fe has a distinct identity and it has steadfastly maintained elements of its cultural heritage. It has a pride in its past as evidenced by many historical markers and monuments and through its 1957 Historical Zoning Ordinance which limits new buildings in the downtown historic area to Pueblo and Territorial styles of architecture. Santa Fe has strong cultural underpinnings with its Indian Pueblo ties, its Hispanic heritage, and its American linkage since its days as the western terminus of the famed Santa Fé Trail. Saint John's College, established in 1696 in Annapolis, Maryland, also has a campus here. Saint John's is rightfully proud of its "Great Books" curriculum, which is unique in American higher education.

Santa Fe epitomizes the bonding that Americans have with the strongest cultural elements of the Southwest. It is a curious fact that this is the capital of the only area in the nation where the Anglo-American onslaught has not subjugated, if not quite effaced, other cultures upon impact. When Americans come to this setting, they are in some mysterious way swayed into a new path and are swirled into a new mode. It is in Santa Fe where Americans adopt a distinctive style of life with its own cuisine, apparel, architecture, and art.

The spirit incarnate of Santa Fe is its plaza. All elements of its society are drawn to this core as if impelled by a powerful magnet. The *Governor's Palace,* the oldest public building in the nation, spans the entire northern side of the plaza. This structure was completed one decade *before* the Pilgrims even landed on the East Coast! The building is a museum piece, both internally and externally. Beneath its long *portal* hover Indians with their cultural

Indians sell their silver and turquoise jewelry to tourists under the portal *of the Governor's Palace at Santa Fe. Photograph by Cotton Mather.*

wares, and passersby pause with an apparent cognizance of the historic roots and the cultural richness embodied in this place. In this plaza by the Governor's Palace are held great fiestas, religious processions, and art fairs, and where individuals and couples absorb the scene from their restful bench positions.

The city's setting is at the southern base of the Sangre de Cristo Mountains. The winding and irregular streets somehow lead to the city center. At this center are the *La Fonda* (which was once a Harvey House, a restaurant chain associated with the railroad), the *Museum of Fine Arts,* the *Cathedral of St. Francis,* and the *Federal Building.* Near the southeast corner of the plaza is *Canyon Road* with its many galleries, shops, and some restaurants, Another significant attraction is the *Museum of International Folk Art* at 706 Camino Lejo. Some people go to the *Downs* of Santa Fe on the south edge of the city, where there is warm-season thoroughbred and quarter horse racing.

Santa Fe has outstanding restaurants and many motels and hotels, ranging from economy lodging to luxury accommodations. Many are on the bustling *Cerillos Road*, a main (though attractive) thoroughfare, leading southwest from the city center past the *Institute of American Indian Arts* and shopping malls and a long strip of gas stations and a motley assortment of highway businesses. Some of Santa Fe's finest accommodations, however, are within a few blocks of the plaza. Despite the abundance of accommodations, Santa Fe has throngs of tourists. Reservations are advisable.

Departing Santa Fe to visit the two renowned Indian Pueblos of *San Ildefonso* and *Santa Clara,* we follow the Bishop's Lodge Road. *Bishop's Lodge,* at the northern fringe of Santa Fe, is a long-established and rather pricey resort with tennis courts and spacious grounds. Farther on is the village of *Tesuque,* an art and wood-carving center.

Twelve miles from Santa Fe, the Bishop's Lodge Road joins U.S. Highways 84 and 285. We follow U.S. Highways 84 and 285 approximately 10 miles to the north, and then take State Highway 502 to the west for 6 miles to the short, clearly marked turnoff to the north which leads to nearby San Ildefonso Pueblo.

San Ildefonso Pueblo and Santa Clara Pueblo, 18 miles, Highways 84/285 and 502

San Ildefonso Pueblo has about 540 persons and 26,191 acres of landholdings. Near the entrance of the Pueblo is a building where tourists are instructed to register and pay a small fee for permission to take photographs (although some areas are off-limits for photography).

The ancestors of San Ildefonso Pueblo were Anasazi people at Mesa Verde who migrated here via Frijoles Canyon (Bandelier

The church at San Ildefonso Pueblo in 1991. Photograph by George F. Thompson.

National Monument). San Ildefonso was established about 1600 and, by 1650, had a population in excess of its present total. The mission was founded in 1617, but the old church was torn down; the present church is a twentieth-century structure.

San Ildefonso is one of the most attractive of all the Pueblos and is famous as the former home of the internationally recognized María Martínez (b. ca. 1886; d. 1980), her husband, Julián (d. 1943), and her son, Popovi Da (b. 1923; d. 1971)—all renowned potters.

Pottery is sold at shops near the plaza and also at some houses that display "pottery for sale" signs. West of the church is the tribal office complex with a small museum that displays some pottery.

Pottery is still made using traditional methods. Special clay is obtained from prized deposits in the hills. The individual pot is

María Martínez, the famous potter of San Ildefonso Pueblo, in the summer of 1972. Photograph by Cotton Mather.

formed from coils of clay which are smoothed with a stone that is handed down from mother to daughter over successive generations. After the pot is formed, it is air-dried. A slip is applied and then it is further dried. Afterward, it is decorated and finally fired. The pottery is red before firing. If it is to remain red, it is fired with an oxidizing flame. If a black finish is desired, it is partially smothered in the firing in a covering of fine, loose manure. Traditional methods did not involve the use of a potter's wheel or a kiln, but now some pottery is being made according to these innovations and not by the traditional methods. Experienced collectors are careful to note this aspect and are aware of the qualitative differences.

The people of San Ildefonso Pueblo are divided into two societal groups, each with its own rectangular ceremonial chambers. The winter people are on the north; the summer people on the south. Public dances in native costumes are held on the plaza, east of the church. A giant cottonwood tree dominates this plaza, and nearby is a ceremonial *kiva*. The public dances are held on January 23, June 13, and September 16. These dances commemorate fertility in people, plants, and animals.

To get to nearby *Santa Clara Pueblo,* return to State Highway 502, turn right and go about 2 miles (across the Rio Grande, that ever-present river), then turn right onto State Highway 30. Seven miles ahead, just beyond the junction to the Puye Cliff Dwellings, turn right again and proceed into Santa Clara Pueblo.

The *Puye Cliff Dwellings,* 11 miles west of State Highway 30, were the site of an Anasazi, cliff-dwelling village established in the early fifteenth century. The road ascends into a beautiful pine forest, with attractive picnic grounds alongside a lovely mountain creek. This is part of the lands of the Santa Clara Indians.

Black Mesa is the prominent igneous landmark between San Ildefonso and Santa Clara Pueblos. Indian legends abound about this mesa, on which are village ruins and pit houses. Black Mesa is off-limits to non-members of these Pueblos.

Santa Clara has approximately 1,450 persons and 45,744 acres of landholdings. The Pueblo has administrative offices and a church (photographs taken of the church's cemetery are not permitted), but no stores or shops. While Santa Clara Pueblo is much larger than San Ildefonso, it is more relaxed and open to visitors.

The best way to visit Santa Clara is to park your vehicle in the open space about a block south of the church and then stroll around. Not only is this less obtrusive, it will also enable you to appreciate the nature of the Pueblo. The Pueblo's older houses are near the center of the settlement. Newer houses, at the Pueblo periphery, usually have departed from the form of flat roofs supported with *vigas,* and with thick adobe walls.

Santa Clara Pueblo is noted for its high-quality pottery. Santa Clara produces the same type of red and black pottery as San Ildefonso. In addition, Santa Clara is prized for its carved pottery. Teresita Naranjo (b. 1918) makes the finest of all carved pottery. Her pottery is much in demand, is sold exclusively from her home, and goes to international collectors. Much of it is sold on order, before it is even made. Fine pottery is a form of fine art, and it commands prices accordingly. However, one can purchase high-quality pieces at the Pueblo at prices below those in Santa Fe or elsewhere. To purchase directly, simply wander through the Pueblo and knock at doors of houses that display "pottery for sale" signs. Prices in the Pueblo are generally realistic, and should be accepted as such.

Most of the pottery in all the Pueblos except San Ildefonso is made and sold by women; at San Ildefonso, much pottery is made by men as well as by women. This is attributed to the fact that both María and Julián Martínez, and their son, Popovi Da, were so instrumental in the revival of pottery as an Indian art form. As noted earlier, most of the high-quality Indian pottery is produced in the Pueblos of Acoma, Hopi, San Ildefonso, San Juan, Santa Clara, and Zia. In general, one pays a premium at San Ildefonso for the same type and quality as that found at Santa Clara. This is a consequence of the tourists' proclivity for obtaining a ceramic piece from the Pueblo that was the home of the famous María. Unfortunately, Acoma Pueblo has become highly commercialized and crowded with tourists; also, much of the pottery there is made non-traditionally, is of deplorable value and abysmal quality, and is marketed at the Pueblo to naive tourists.

A Santa Clara Pueblo woman bakes bread in an outdoor oven. Photograph by Cotton Mather.

An adobe structure at Santa Clara Pueblo, with wooden vigas, *falls into ruins in the late summer of 1968. Photograph by Cotton Mather.*

Eusebia Shije of Zia Pueblo holds one of her pots in the summer of 1978. She remains one of the Southwest's most accomplished ceramic artists. Photograph by Cotton Mather.

Significantly, most of the men at Santa Clara, San Ildefonso, San Juan, and other nearby Pueblos are employed in Los Alamos or Santa Fe, and, thus, they do a lot of commuting to and from home and work. The economy of the Pueblos is heavily dependent upon the income of both women and men, and material goods such as VCRs and television sets have become increasingly a part of Pueblo Indians' life and ambitions. There is also concern that there may be a relationship between the high incidence of cancer at Santa Clara Pueblo, in particular, and the nuclear complex at Los Alamos, upriver.

Upon departure from Santa Clara to *Chimayó* turn right (north) on State Highway 30 and go 2 miles into Española. In Española, turn right and cross the Rio Grande and then turn left (north) on U.S. Highway 285. Proceed to State Highway 76, then turn right (east) and go east on this road for 9 miles up the *Santa Cruz Valley* to Chimayó.

Santa Cruz, New Mexico, to Chimayó, New Mexico, 11 miles, Highways 30 and 285

The village of *Santa Cruz,* 2.5 miles from the junction of U.S. Highway 285 and State Highway 76, is just to the left of our route. It was established in 1695 by sixty families from Zacatecas, Mexico, as La Villa Nueva de Santa Cruz de los Españoles Mexicanos del Rey Nuestra Señor Don Carlos Segundo (The New Town of the Holy Cross of the Spanish Mexicans of the King of Our Master Don Carlos II). Mercifully, the village's name has been shortened.

Santa Cruz, a quiet settlement dominated by a huge church built in 1733, has a turbulent history. The interior of the church contains early Spanish-American art and woodcarving.

The *Santa Cruz Valley,* east of the village of Santa Cruz, has many adobe houses and small fields of chiles, *frijoles* (beans), vegetables, corn, and some peach and apple orchards. The small landholdings in this valley just a few decades ago were semi-subsistence farms. Today, they are homesteads of families supported chiefly by employment in Santa Fe and Los Alamos.

The renowned Spanish-American weaver, John Trujillo, at his loom in Chimayó, New Mexico, in the summer of 1978. Photograph by Cotton Mather.

Chimayó is well-known for the weaving shop of John Trujillo, for Rancho de Chimayó, and because of El Santuario de Chimayó. Chimayó is the Tewa Indian description (*tsimayo*) for the "good flaking stone" that is abundant in the surrounding hills.

John Trujillo's Weaving Shop is in a small building on the left. Señor Trujillo is a tall, gentle man with a dignified and engaging personality. His weavings are superb and are known nationally from coast to coast and internationally. He is an authority of the history of this weaving center, which has been producing fine hand-loomed textiles since the early eighteenth century. Many wayfarers also visit Ortega's shop, which is just around the corner on the right (follow the sign for *Rancho de Chimayó*).

A turn to the right, just beyond Trujillo's shop, leads to Rancho de Chimayó and its *restaurante* and *hacienda*. This is one of the finest Hispanic eating establishments in the Southwest. Reservations are recommended (telephone 505-351-4444; closed in January and some Mondays). It is operated by the Jaramillo family (residents of Chimayó since the 1700s who trace their roots to the first Spanish settlers) in a restored (October of 1965) old adobe hacienda which has a series of pleasant outdoor terraces.

In August of 1984, the Jaramillo family completed restoration of Hacienda Rancho de Chimayó, a country inn in the old family home of Epifanio and Adelaida Jaramillo across the road from the *restaurante*. This delightful bed-and-breakfast facility has seven lovely guest rooms. Each room opens onto an enclosed courtyard, and each room is comfortably furnished with antiques of this locale. Here, too, reservations are advisable (telephone 505-351-2222; closed in January).

The Santuario de Chimayó is a short distance beyond Rancho de Chimayó on the left. The church, constructed in 1813 to 1816, is known throughout the region for the reputed healing power of the earth in the room to the left of the altar. Pilgrims walk for miles on Easter to this shrine and then toss braces and crutches aside in testimony to the curative power of the holy earth. During the Gulf War in the winter of 1991, many pictures of local soldiers who were stationed overseas graced the walls of this room. Messages of "I love you" and "Return home safely" brought an energy to the room that few visitors could deny. New Mexicans have always been represented in the armed services in large numbers.

The easiest return to Santa Fe is to continue on scenic State Highway 503 and thence onward via U.S. Highway 285.

△ Day Four

SANTA FE, NEW MEXICO, TO DURANGO, COLORADO, 208 MILES

On the morning of the fourth day we go north 147 miles on U.S. Highway 84 to Pagosa Springs, Colorado. This takes us via Española, thence 30 miles along the colorful Chama Valley, past the Ghost Ranch, through the tragic town of Tierra Amarilla, on to the headquarters for hunters and fishers at the town of Chama, thence to the tourist center of Pagosa Springs. Our afternoon route is via U.S. Highway 160 through rugged terrain to Durango.

Santa Fe, New Mexico, to Abiquiú, New Mexico, 42 miles, Highway 84

We move quickly northward from Santa Fe over the four-lane U.S. Highway 84 to *Española* (5,600 feet). From Española to Abiquiú (5,930 feet) we stay on U.S. Highway 84 and follow closely the *Chama River*, a tributary of the Río Bravo del Norte (Rio Grande). This 18-mile stretch of the Chama River has numerous diversion irrigation dams, and some barbed-wire fences are strung across the stream; this discourages river boaters. However, the upper Chama River, between Abiquiú and the El Vado Reservoir, flows through spectacular scenery and is fine for boating.

Most of the settlement from Española to Abiquiú is on the alluvial land of the Chama River. The desultory agriculture and the low yields do not make this a prosperous area. Part-time farming

Santa Fe, New Mexico, to Durango, Colorado

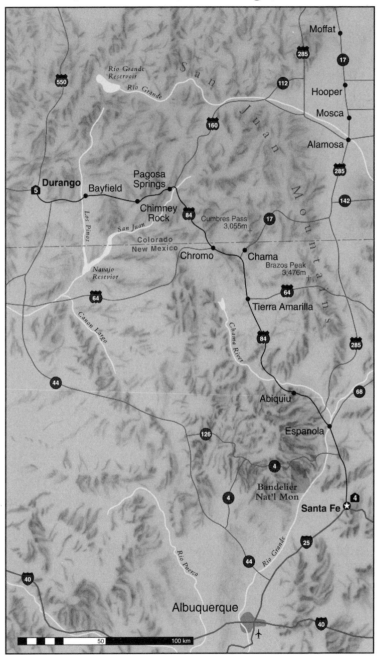

prevails and much of the population depends upon food stamps or some other form of government aid. Houses are modest and there are many "mobile homes."

The mesa south of Abiquiú is capped by Tertiary basalt.

Abiquiú, New Mexico, to Tierra Amarillo, New Mexico, 44 miles, Highway 84

Two miles before reaching Abiquiú, a dirt road leads east (to the right) to *Ghost Ranch,* an adult study-center operated by the United Presbyterian Church. Formerly a working ranch that painter Georgia O'Keeffe first visited in 1935, it is now a seminar center for the community with emphasis on conservation, cultural topics, and community organization. The curious name of Ghost Ranch was derived from reports that witches (*brujas*) inhabited the canyons. The Ghost Ranch is backed by Jurassic sandstone bluffs which top Triassic deposits with many specimens of the dinosaur *Coelophysis.*

Abiquiú is a village whose early inhabitants were Spanish and *genizaros,* captive Indians who took Spanish surnames and customs. Spanish settlement was initiated here in 1744, but life was hazardous because of Ute, Comanche, Apache, and Navajo raids. Notwithstanding, *Abiquiú* had nearly 1,800 people by the year 1800.

The Spanish-American Pedro Gonzales acquired many small parcels of land in the mid-1800s. Later, his son, Miguel, further expanded the family landholdings and developed a huge sheep-ranching operation. Fifteen of his sheep camps had an estimated 150,000 sheep. Some small landholders, however, persisted as farmers, but with little net income. Increasingly, the local men became seasonal laborers in distant mines and lumber camps or sheepherders in Colorado and Utah. The Great Depression of the 1930s was especially harsh for people in Abiquiú. Some residents moved away. Others had farms of only four acres at a time when Miguel Gonzales owned 60 percent of the floodplain in Abiquiú's land grant. The small landholders were in poverty. The relief rolls expanded.

Then came the Muslims in the 1980s. They established a foundation with considerable financial support from Saudi Arabia and acquired 8,000 acres within a decade.

The outside world has added other elements to Abiquiú. Spanish-American residents commute long distances to work at Española, Los Alamos, and Santa Fe. Some Anglo-American retirees have moved into the community. Tourists come to see the former home of Georgia O'Keeffe, who bought her first house in the area in 1940 at Ghost Ranch and then another home in town in 1945. She lived in Abiquiú permanently after her husband, the famous artist/photographer Alfred Stieglitz, died in 1946. She passed away in 1986. About 600,000 people annually visit the Abiquiú Dam reservoir. Today, Abiquiú has approximately 500 residents. What does tomorrow bring? Alvar W. Carlson, in his book *The Spanish-American Homeland,* devotes an entire chapter to Abiquiú, and he raises the question of whether Abiquiú can remain a Spanish-American community.

Our travel on U.S. Highway 84 continues for 30 miles beyond Abiquiú through spectacular canyon country with bold cliffs and intricate erosional forms that have brilliant red and yellow coloration. The route leaves the Chama River about 7 miles north of Abiquiú. Near this point, on a steep hill, a small highway "pull-off" enables you to park and revel over one of the most spectacular views of the Chama River in its gorge. Of this country and of O'Keeffe's love of New Mexico (the Land of Enchantment), she wrote the following in January of 1939 (as quoted in *Georgia O'Keeffe in the West,* edited by Doris Bry and Nicholas Callaway [1989]):

A red hill doesn't touch everyone's heart as it touches mine and I suppose there is no reason why it should. The red hill is a piece of the bad lands where even the grass is gone. Bad lands roll away outside my door—hill after hill—red hill of apparently the same sort of earth that you mix with oil to make paint. All the earth colors of the painter's palette are out there in the many miles of bad lands.

Twenty miles beyond Abiquiú is the *Ghost Ranch Living Museum* in the Carson National Forest. The museum has geology exhibits, small animals of the region in pens, plus some large animals, including elk and mountain lion. This is an informative rest stop, open daily from 800 to 1730, April 15 until September 1; open the rest of the year from 800 to 1630. There is an admission charge. The land for this center was exchanged for title to land claimed by 111 families who had lived here for generations and had struggled bitterly for clear land ownership.

Just after leaving the Ghost Ranch Living Museum, a dirt road leads westward (to the left) to the *Christ in the Desert Monastery.* This is a Benedictine monastery, 13 miles off the highway, where the monks cultivate gardens, make pottery, do woodworking, and operate a guest house.

From a point 19 miles beyond Abiquiú, we travel to Tierra Amarilla, another 20 miles over a high plateau (about 7,600 feet) that is alternately forest and rangeland outside the Carson National Forest. The forest has been heavily lumbered and the remaining timber is a rather short stand of piñon and juniper. The sparsely populated upland is popular among hunters because of its deer, elk, and bear.

At the junction of U.S. Highways 84 and 64, we turn right and enter *Tierra Amarilla* (7,520 feet). The economically depressed town is in a topographic depression at the confluence of the *Río Brazos,* the *Río Chama,* and the *Río de Tierra Amarilla.* The adjacent uplands rise to 10,712 feet at a peak 8 miles to the east. Three miles north of this peak is the 2,000-foot-deep *Brazos Box,* or Brazos Canyon, where the Río Brazos has formed badlands and a deep canyon incised into Precambrian sedimentary rock. A lava flow from small cinder cones to the northeast tumbled into Brazos Box 250,000 to 1,000,000 years ago; this lava flow reaches U.S. Highway 84 north of Tierra Amarilla.

Tierra Amarilla ("Yellow Earth") was not established permanently until the arrival of U.S. troops in the 1840s. Settlement was slow, however, because of Indian raids by Ute, Jicarilla Apache, and Navajo. Since 1880 it has been the county seat or political capital of Arriba County, in this native Río Arriba region. Until recent decades this area of Spanish-American settlement was supported almost solely by subsistence agriculture. The region has been isolated by both topography and regional culture. Today, it is a problem area. Controversies abound over land titles, the U.S. Forest Service's livestock-grazing permits, and the economic plight. In *The Spanish-American Homeland,* Professor Carlson presents an insightful analysis of the roots of settlement, the aspects of poverty, the administration of land use in the national forest, as well as the architecture, religion, and the vernacular landscape. Also of use is *Community and Continuity: The History, Architecture, and Cultural Landscape of La Tierra Amarilla,* by Chris Wilson and David Kammer (1989), which is especially strong in its analysis of the area's architecture as well as its irrigation and field patterns.

The nation's attention was focused in 1957 on Tierra Amarilla because of a shootout at the courthouse. This stemmed from Reis Lopez Tijerina's organization, named the Alianza Federal de los Mercedes (Federal Alliance for Land Grants), and the military attempt to return lands to descendants of the original Spanish-American settlers. The Alianza claimed reparations for alleged injustices by the federal government and compensation for past profits from these lands. Also, the Alianza manifested antipathy for Anglo-American cultural and political influence, notwithstanding the Spanish-American dominance of political offices at the local and state levels and with their own representatives in the U.S. Congress. Tijerina was later arrested and incarcerated for two years.

Tierra Amarilla is now in a rather moribund state with a diminishing population, buildings in general disrepair, and windows boarded up. Residents subsist with the help of their gardens, a few cows, and the government's food stamps.

The route from Tierra Amarilla to Chama, about 8 miles south of the Colorado-New Mexico state line, is along a valley with hay land and ranchsteads. The forested highlands to the east (right) rise to 11,403 feet. Sheep and cattle are raised mostly in the valley and on the less elevated upland to the west.

Chama, New Mexico, to Durango, Colorado, 104 miles, Highways 84 and 160

Chama (a Spanish approximation of the Tewa *tzama,* "here they wrestled") has a population of 1,098, unless the Saturday night bar addicts are included. The town got its start as a trade center for the sheep and cattle ranches. Then a boom was born in 1879 with plans for a narrow-gauge railroad from *Antonito,* Colorado, 49 miles to the east-northeast, over *Cumbres Pass* (10,022 feet), to Chama (7,860 feet). By 1880, the population exceeded 1,000. Laborers appeared in droves and vanished almost as suddenly for the gold and silver camps to the northwest in the San Juan Mountains. Men were in demand by the railroad for surveying, grading, building bridges and tunnels, cutting ties, and laying track. The first train arrived in Chama on 12 December 1880, and the town boomed until the Great Depression of the 1930s. Then, prices plunged, sheepmen went broke, the railway gave way to trucks now moving over the paved roads, and the famous Volstead Act of 1919 was repealed.

The legislatures of New Mexico and Colorado voted in 1970 to purchase and resuscitate the railroad. Now the quaint *Cumbres and Toltec Scenic Railroad* (C. & T.R.R.) operates a century-old, coal-burning, steam-powered train from mid-June until mid-October. Thousands of tourists travel this beautiful route each year. (The regular car route via Highway 17 is equally beautiful.) The optimum time for the trip is about October 1st when, amidst the evergreens, are set the golden leaves of the aspen trees. Then one can whiff away the smoke of bygone times, flick away the engine soot and cares of yesteryears, and view this line as a sublime return to instead times! Reservations for the train tour are recommended (contact the Cumbres and Toltec Scenic Railroad, P.O. Box 789, Chama, New Mexico 87520, U.S.A. or telephone 505-756-2151).

Few travelers will confuse Chama, New Mexico, with Vail, Colorado. Note Chama's unused livestock pens rotting alongside the railway, the town's many log structures, the old stores, the archaic hotel accommodations, the rustic cabins, and the

SIDE TRIP TO MONERO AND LUMBERTON

A side trip for ghost town devotees can be had by proceeding 4 miles west on U.S. Highway 64 to *Monero,* New Mexico, where coal was initially mined in 1881 as the Denver and Rio Grande Railroad was being laid from Chama, New Mexico, to Durango, Colorado. Monero means "money" in Italian, and a number of Italians lived in the town when it was first established, so that may account for the town's name. Another account attributes the name to a bureaucratic blunder. Supposedly a typographical error was made by the U.S. Post Office Department when it received the town name of *Minero,* which means "miner" in Spanish. Either way, both words fit the ambitions of the times and the kind of work. Monero's population peaked in the 1930s when the two large coal mines and several smaller ones were very active, even twenty-four hours a day, we are told. But the mines closed by the 1960s, the post office shut its doors in 1963 (without resolving the issue of the town's real name), and the trains are gone. Today Monero is, sad but true, a ghastly ghost town with only a few buildings left standing.

No doubt this visit will really charge some of your batteries, so to see more proceed another 5 miles west of Monero on 64 to *Lumberton,* New Mexico, which was named about 1894 for the many sawmills in the vicinity. With the coming of the Denver and Rio Grande Railroad in 1881, timber was needed as the rails were being laid. Thus, a big-time lumber industry developed in the Chama Valley. One of the largest sawmill operators at that time was a Mr. E. M. Biggs, who bought forty acres from a ranch owned by Señor Francisco Lobato. Biggs then surveyed the streets and lots, and he had himself a modern town. The town's original name was *Amargo,* which means "bitter" in Spanish, apparently in tribute to the taste of the town's river water. By World War I, the area had been completely cleared of its timber and, according to the *Roadside History of New Mexico,* old-timers claimed that the area from Lumberton to Chama "was a forest of rotting stumps." Although the post office still operates (as of this writing), and ranching and oil production occur in the area, we have in Lumberton a ghost town of forest denudation. There was no such thing as forest ecology, land-use management and planning, or a "green movement" in the old days—just progress.

Return east to Monero and back to the junction of U.S. Highway 64 and U.S. Highway 84. Then turn left (head north) to *Pagosa Springs,* Colorado.

---

billboards and real estate signs. A visit here is truly motivation for travel (though chatter in the local cafe can be interesting), so push on to Pagosa Springs, Colorado, staying on U.S. Highway 84.

Ten miles west of Chama, we cross the *Continental Divide* (7,766 feet). Four miles farther is the junction of U.S. Highways 64 and 84. We continue of U.S. Highway 84, to the right (north), to Pagosa Springs.

En route to *Chromo,* Colorado, just over the state line and 24 miles northwest of Chama, we travel through some of the finest big game country in the United States. Here is ranchland with magnificent highland pastures, edged by beautiful, bold bluffs and in sight of the towering peaks of the *San Juan Mountains.* Herefords and Angus dot the pastures. The scene is serene. When autumn comes, hunters appear with four-wheel-drive vehicles topped with "campers" and pulling horse trailers. Horses are the hunter's solution for packing big game trophies out of the rugged terrain.

Chromo has two buildings, a residence, plus a store that sells hunting licenses. The suburban section is comprised of an abandoned home and a relict schoolhouse ready for restoration. Our correspondents from near Chromo inform us that most of the hunters come from Texas, Oklahoma, Arkansas, Louisiana, and California.

A stretch of our route, about 10 miles south of Pagosa Springs, follows a sparkling stream, the *Río Blanco*. Many cabins line the banks. The large sawmill, 8 miles from Pagosa Springs, is cutting wood for log houses, the new fashion in architecture from the Southern to Northern Rocky Mountains.

Pagosa Springs (7,095 feet) has scenic surroundings that are sprouting sumptuous houses. Land prices here have soared. Pagosa Springs, the county seat of Archuleta County, has doubled its population in the past half century to its present total of 1,482.

Pagosa Springs ("Healing Waters") derives its name from spring water heated by rocks of Tertiary and Quaternary (recent) age. Formerly, the springs were contentiously used by both the Navajo and Ute Indians. The main hot spring, one of the largest in the United States, discharges 700 gallons per minute and is used to heat some buildings.

The town, established in 1880, is set in the western part of a shale-based valley bounded by hills and *cuestas* (hills, slopes, or ridges with a steep face on one side and a gentle slope on the other) of Cretaceous sandstones. Early on, Pagosa Springs had service on the Denver and Rio Grande Railroad and became a lumbering and ranch trade center. The sparkling clear *San Juan River,* which has public fishing stretches alongside and is known for its brown and rainbow trout, flows through town.

Turn left in Pagosa Springs onto U.S. Highway 160 and proceed 55 miles westward to Durango, Colorado.

Pagosa Springs is a good town for replenishing travelers' supplies, although modern lodging accommodations are limited. One comfortable motel is in town and an alternative is the Fairfield Pagosa Resort, 3.5 miles west on U.S. Highway 160. The resort has a small private lake, a lodge with restaurant, some condominiums, and an attractive golf course (so important these days) with pleasant views of the San Juan Mountains.

West of Pagosa Springs, the highway crosses a high anticline of Dakota Sandstone. The volcanic *San Juan Mountains,* visible to the north, are bounded on all but the east by (Paleozoic and

Mesozoic) sedimentary rocks which form asymmetrical (cuestaform) ridges. At the town of *Chimney Rock,* 17 miles west of Pagosa Springs, is a "hogback," or a steeply inclined cuestaform ridge.

Chimney Rock's name is from a nearby rock formation on a high mesa with ancient Indian ruins. These ruins are now administered as a national historic site. They were once the home of 2,000 Anasazi people.

About 5 miles west of Chimney Rock, we cross the Piedra ("Rock") River, a clear mountain stream. The *Upper Piedra,* 20 miles from a bridge north of Pagosa Springs to the bridge on U.S. Highway 160 that is west of Chimney Rock, courses through canyons where portages are impossible. This is a thrilling section for expert kayakers and no place for novices. The *Lower Piedra,* a 10-mile stretch above the Navajo Reservoir, is quiet and peaceful as it meanders by *alamosas* (cottonwoods) and through ranchland.

Just west of the U.S. Highway 160 bridge over the Piedra River is the Piedra post office and general store with gas and groceries. The summer tourist business is from June until September. Hunters come in the fall, challenging one's right to arm bears. The rest of the year is peaceful.

The middle third of the route from Pagosa Springs to Durango is through dissected terrain in the *San Juan National Forest.* The highway in this section is at an elevation of 6,800 to 7,800 feet; nearby uplands peak at 10,540 feet. Antelope, deer, elk, and some bear roam this upland.

Bayfield (6,500 feet) is a small settlement, 19 miles from Durango on the north-south flowing *Los Pinos River*, a tributary of the San Juan River. Both east and west of Bayfield are some new oil wells, but there is no other industry at Bayfield. Residents number about one person for every 20 feet of elevation above sea level, and it is a little-known fact that, in this respect, Bayfield, Colorado, as distinct from its sister city, Bayfield, Wisconsin, on the shores of Lake Superior, surpasses Rotterdam, the birthplace of the famous Dutch painter, Pieter de Hooch (b. 1629; d. after 1683 or 1684).

We conclude our travel day at *Durango*, the largest urban center in the southwestern quarter of Colorado. Durango is the home of Fort Lewis College, but that is not what attracts tourists to Durango.

Durango, Colorado, to Kayenta, Arizona

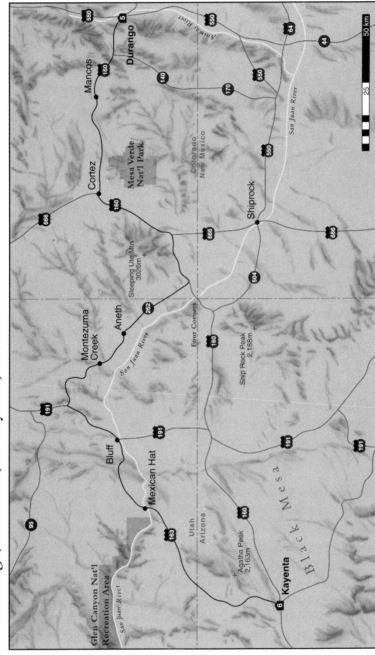

△ *Day Five*

DURANGO, COLORADO, TO KAYENTA, ARIZONA, 233 MILES

Our fifth day is on the Colorado Plateau and starts from Durango with a short drive west on U.S. Highway 160 and then south to Mesa Verde National Park, one of the greatest places in the U.S. West. After visiting Mesa Verde, we lunch at Cortez and proceed via the San Juan River through the southeastern corner of Utah and Monument Valley to the outpost of Kayenta.

Durango, Colorado, to Cortez, Colorado, 46 miles, Highway 160

Durango (6,505 feet) is the seat of government of La Plata County. Its population has approximately doubled in the past half century to its present total of 13,462. True, Durango is not as populous as Philadelphia on the East Coast or even Keokuk on the banks of the mighty Mississippi, but it is the reigning urban center of southwestern Colorado.

Founded in 1880 by the Denver and Rio Grande Railroad, Durango has had a riotous past rooted in mining and smelting and as a brawling haven for cowboys on the loose. Now Durango's economic base is tourism, although it is also the home of *Fort Lewis (State) College*, with a 1990 enrollment of 3,984 students and a faculty of 180. This coeducational institution, founded in

A cowboy with his packhorse keeps "them doggies movin'" 32 miles west of Durango, Colorado. Photograph by Cotton Mather.

1911, offers a bachelor's degree plus a really fine physical setting on a ledge overlooking Durango.

Attractive scenery surrounds Durango. Tourists enjoy going northward over the spectacular *Million Dollar Highway* (U.S. Highway 550) to the old mining center of *Ouray* and *Silverton* or to ride on the narrow-gauge, coal-burning train to Silverton, or to engage in white-water rafting on the *Animas River*. For travel on the Durango & Silverton Narrow Gauge Railroad, reservations are strongly advised (telephone 303-247-2733). Some tourists prefer the dude ranches and riding horseback in the scenic *San Juan Mountains*. (For information on pack trips, telephone Purgatory Resort: 303-247-9000.) But the most appealing attraction is *Mesa Verde National Park*.

South of Durango is the decades-old, proposed Animas River—La Plata River Project. This $589 million scheme would include two reservoirs, three major pumping plants, and a 157-mile network of pipes and canals that would irrigate 68,000 acres. The proposal is controversial because of critical questions pertaining to the rare Colorado squawfish and razorback suckers. Also in dispute are the water rights and pork barrels. The Navajo maintain that the project will give some of their water to the Ute.

West of Durango, our route goes up a canyon bordered by uplands capped with Mesaverde Sandstone of Cretaceous age. The sedimentary rock north of our highway is tilted upward toward the San Juan Mountains. Underlying the Mesaverde Sandstone is the Mancos Shale, which is slippery when wet; thus, landslides are common in this area.

Twelve miles west of Durango we observe one of the most striking vegetative changes, from tall forest to rangeland and scrubby piñon pine and juniper.

Thirteen miles onward, take the business route into *Mancos* (6,993 feet), one of the oldest coal-mining towns in western Colorado. This pleasant town (population 912) has a "western" look. What supports such a town today? Note the huge sawmill at the western limit of the town. Timber is trucked in from miles around. (The *San Juan National Forest* is to the north and east.) Also, just 5 miles west of Mancos, on the left, observe the broad sweep of *Mancos Valley* that is in hay and pasture. This is a fine beef area where Herefords, Angus, and crossbred cattle prevail.

Westward 7.6 miles from Mancos, we leave U.S. Highway 160 and go south 21 miles from the entrance to the *Mesa Verde National Park* headquarters and the *Chapin Mesa ruins.*

The Anasazi inhabited this area for about 1,000 years, and Mesa Verde is thought to be the heart of their dominion. Mesa Verde National Park is our largest archeological preserve and it has the most cliff dwellings ever discovered in our land. Researchers have located nearly 4,000 archeological sites in the park and more than 600 of these are cliff dwellings. Mesa Verde was one of the first sites in the world selected by UNESCO (United Nations

Visitors armed with videocameras and self-guided tour brochures ex-
plore the Cliff Palace ruins at Mesa Verde National Park in gorgeous fall
weather. Photograph by George F. Thompson.

Education, Scientific, and Cultural Organization) to be a World
Heritage Cultural Site.

The highest elevation on the Mesa Verde is 8,572 feet. The mesa
slopes to 6,000 feet in the south and has serrate edges where
erosion has moved headward into the upland. The oldest exposed
rock is the Mancos Shale, a gray limy formation, topped with
Mesaverde Sandstone.

Mesa Verde has 14 to 18 inches of average annual precipitation;
of this amount, about 80 to 100 inches are in the form of snow
(remember that 1 inch of rain equals about 8 to 14 inches of snow).
Winter travel is sometimes blocked.

A father and his young son climb out of the Cliff Palace ruins via the steep Anasazi-like ladders at Mesa Verde National Park. Photograph by George F. Thompson.

Piñon pine and juniper dominate the vegetation of the Mesa Verde. At the highest elevations are some stands of Douglas fir (*Pseudotsuga taxifolia*). And parallel to the north rim, several miles to the south, is a mountain-brush association of Gambel oak (*Quercus gambelii* nutt.), Saskatoon serviceberry (*Amelanchier alnifolia* [Nutt.] Nutt.), Utah serviceberry (*Amelanchier utahensis koehne*), and mountain mahogany (*Cercocarpus intricatus wats.*)—a haunt for mule deer—that are also found in Utah's magnificent Zion National Park, 250 miles to the west as the magpie flies.

Wild animals of the Mesa Verde include the mule deer, cougar (mountain lion), coyote, gray fox, bighorn sheep, bobcat, badger, squirrel, chipmunk, porcupine, rabbit, lizard, and rattlesnake. Visitors bent on wildlife photography are advised to respect the latter.

Who discovered Mesa Verde after its abandonment? Some historians attribute this to William Henry Jackson (b. 1843; d. 1942) in 1874. He was in command of the Photographic Division of the U.S. Geological and Geographical Survey of the Territories and was a renowned photographer himself. Most credit, however, is given to the Quaker family of Benjamin K. Wetherill (d. 1898), who in 1881 settled 3 miles southwest of Mancos. Benjamin and his five sons rapidly expanded their ranch and they were friendly to the Ute Indians. One of the sons, Richard, and his brother-in-law, Charles Mason, while looking for some stray cattle on 18 December 1888, encountered the Cliff Palace ruins. In subsequent years, the Wetherills collected thousands of artifacts and publicized their collection. Their first large collection was sold to the Colorado State Historical Society in Denver. Their second notable sale was to the C. D. Hazard and Jay Smith Exploring Company, which exhibited it at the Chicago World's Fair (The World's Columbian Exposition) in 1893.

Anthropological research indicates that the Anasazi came to Mesa Verde about AD 500. Here they changed from a nomadic existence to one based upon farming supplemented by hunting and gathering. They lived mainly in pithouses on the mesa top. About AD 750, they began to construct houses aboveground, in long and curved rows and facing a pithouse or two. By AD 1000, Anasazi architecture had evolved from adobe-and-pole to stone masonry structures as high as three stories and with several dozen rooms. The classic period of Mesa Verde was AD 1100 to 1300. At that time, the population totaled a few thousand, mostly concentrated in compact settlements and often in sheltered cliff alcoves. The cliff houses were abandoned by AD 1300, perhaps because of drought and depletion of resources. The Anasazi are likely the progenitors of some Pueblo Indians.

The tools of the Anasazi were carefully honed of stone, wood, and bone and were used for cutting, pounding, grinding, scraping, polishing, perforating, and weaving. The Anasazi employed the digging stick in crop culture, the stone axe for land clearance, and the bow and arrow for hunting game. Their basketry was beautifully decorated and was used for toting and for storing grain. The quality of basketry, however, declined as the women learned to make pottery, which was both handsome and functional.

For visitors who are at the park ruins for a bit less than a half day, a feasible plan is to stop at the museum and park headquarters for a half hour. The museum is open 0800 to 1830 in summer and from 0800 to 1700 the rest of the year. Then take the Ruins Road which has two loops of 6 miles each. The loop to the east leads to Balcony House and *Cliff Palace*. The latter is Mesa Verde's largest and most famous ruin. Cliff Palace can be visited as a self-guided tour in summer; allow about one hour. (Note: Those people with heart problems or other physical ailments might wish to avoid this tour, because there is a long, steep descent and an ascent up Anasazi-like ladders.) Cliff Palace is closed in winter.

After returning to the park entrance, go west (left) on U.S. Highway 160 for 10 miles to *Cortez* (6,198 feet). Cortez (population 8,300), founded in 1887, depends heavily on tourism and is experiencing rapid growth. It has some satisfactory food and lodging accommodations. Cortez is, also, a trade center for ranchers, for farmers on nearby irrigated fields, and for Ute Indians.

Continue south from Cortez on U.S. Highway 160 for 32.3 miles (and stay alert in 20 miles when 160 veers to the southwest; don't follow 666 to the south), when we turn right on Colorado Highway 41. At this intersection note the famous *Shiprock Peak* (in Navajo, *tae-bidaki*—the winged rock) that is 24.6 miles to the south-southeast. Shiprock (7,178 feet) is a volcanic rock, with radiating dikes, that rises 1,700 feet above its base. At closer range, one notes the columnar jointing of the igneous material. There are many wonderful Indian legends and stories associated with this landmark. (Note: Twenty miles east of Shiprock Peak is the *Four Corners Power Plant* that burns seven million tons of Cretaceous coal annually and produces 2,085 megawatts of electricity and untold amounts of air pollution. This coal is mined on the Navajo Reservation, and the environmental impact of such mining has created much turmoil and corruption within the Navajo nation. Indians in this area used coal before the advent of the white settler, but not for electrical generation.)

After leaving Cortez, the forest is behind us. The first 10 miles beyond Cortez, to the southwest, is past irrigated cropland, mostly in hay. Then we enter the *Ute Indian Reservation,* a steppe and desert land with almost no habitations visible, just vast stretches of grazing territory that meagerly supports sheep, goats, and a few horses. This is Colorado Plateau country at echelon levels and with a few monumental buttes.

Sleeping Ute Mountain, 11 miles southwest of Cortez, is formed from (Tertiary) magma that was intruded as a laccolith into sedimentary rock around the San Juan Mountains. The sedimentary rock above this magma has now been removed by erosion. The highest point of Sleeping Ute Mountain rises to 9,987 feet, nearly 4,000 feet above its base. The igneous rock has domed up the Mancos Shale (Mesozoic) and overlying Mesaverde Sandstone, but not the lower Dakota Sandstone (Mesozoic). The intersecting lines of Colorado, Utah, New Mexico, and Arizona create the "Four Corners Area," because it is the only point in the U.S. common to four states. *Four Corners* is about 5 miles southwest of the junction of U.S. Highway 160 and State Highway 41; the surface there (above 5,000 feet) is a small plateau of Dakota Sandstone. Take State Highway 41 to the right and proceed toward the Utah border.

Colorado-Utah State Border to Kayenta, Arizona, 106 miles, Highways 41, 262, and 163

About 9 miles after the intersection of U.S. Highway 160 and Colorado Highway 41, we cross the Colorado-Utah border and our road becomes Utah Highway 262. Five miles farther, the land is suddenly more dissected where we descend the bluffs to the valley of the *San Juan River.*

In 3 more miles we are at the few buildings of the *Aneth School* (4,820 feet), a boarding school under the Bureau of Indian Affairs. One mile farther is the Indian town of *Aneth,* which has a few houses and a general store and gas pump.

An oil field is just west-northwest of Aneth. More than a dozen companies hold leases on the *Aneth Oil Field,* which yields more than $2 million annually in royalties and interest. Under a 1933 federal law, Utah Navajo are entitled to 37½ percent of oil royalties in the reservation's Aneth area.

We follow Highway 262 and the San Juan River (to the left) to *Montezuma Creek,* 9 miles beyond the town of Aneth. The town has a grocery store, a huge high school, a few dozen houses and mobile homes, some oil tanks, and a Baptist and a Mormon church. But this is primarily a Navajo community.

We proceed west from Montezuma Creek to Bluff, a distance of 15 miles, on Utah Highway 163, thence onward to Kayenta, Arizona, on U.S. Highway 163.

Bluff (4,500 feet), a village with some Navajo residents, has a population of 100. The scene here is dominated by two remarkable sandstone turrets that rise behind the Twin Rock Trading Post. The village has a Mormon church and modest motel and restaurant accommodations.

This is the most arid section of the Colorado Plateau. Bluff receives less than seven and one-half inches of average annual precipitation. While the summers are hot (temperatures rise to 90 or 100 degrees Fahrenheit), the average temperature in January is 27.9 degrees Fahrenheit, and subzero temperatures occur frequently during the winter.

SIDE TRIP TO HOVENWEEP NATIONAL MONUMENT

On our route, the best way to reach this small, but very impressive site on the Utah-Colorado border is to head northeast directly out of *Aneth* on the only road possible—an unpaved road that, in about 7 miles, will get you to the monument. But please be aware of two matters before you attempt this side trip. First, the road is rough, unpaved though graded, and requires high vehicular clearance (to avoid possible mishaps such as losing a muffler or an oil pan). Second, during the summer, daytime temperatures can be hot, so one must be careful about possible dehydration and sunburn on an extended hike to the ruins.

Hovenweep (a Ute word meaning "deserted valley") comprises six groups of prehistoric masonry towers, cliff dwellings, and pueblos. On the site are many archeological wonders. Although Hovenweep is located on Cajon Mesa, which, according to the *Smithsonian Guide to Historic America* (Volume 10: *The Desert States*), was likely visited by nomadic hunters as far back as 14,000 years ago, the Anasazi in about AD 500 were the first prehistoric people to settle in villages and to grow crops here. Like the Anasazi throughout the region, they stayed until about AD 1300.

There is a modest visitor and ranger center at the *Square Tower Ruin*, which includes the well-preserved *Hovenweep Castle*. Trails lead to the other groups of ruins in the monument, both in Utah and in Colorado. The monument is free and is open daily from 0800 until 1630. (For information about visiting the ruins, contact Area Manager, Hovenweep National Monument, McElmo Route, Cortez, Colorado 81321, U.S.A. or telephone 303-529-4465.)

SIDE TRIP TO CANYONLANDS NATIONAL PARK AND ARCHES NATIONAL PARK

Our route takes us along the southern fringe of the renowned canyonlands of southeastern Utah. Everyone should make the effort to visit Canyonlands National Park, one of the nation's greatest outdoor wonders; and, if you have two days to spend rather than one, you can also visit Arches National Park and travel along State Highway 128 (a scenic byway along the Colorado River) farther to the north. If taking this side trip is impossible, then at least buy a copy of Edward Abbey's book, *Desert Solitaire* (1968; 1988), an enduring work by one of America's most celebrated nature writers. Abbey (b. 1927; d. 1989) worked for sixteen years as a ranger with the National Park Service and National Forest Service, and this book is an account of his time in the "canyonland country" of Utah. The book reflects his profound love of nature and of southeastern Utah and his bitter abhorrence of all who would try to desecrate either of them.

From *Bluff* head north on U.S. Highway 191 about 47 miles to *Monticello,* Utah (7,050 feet), a pleasant Mormon community that we much prefer as a home base than Moab, an additional 84 miles to the north. In Monticello one can now find a new and well-run Days Inn that also offers complimentary continental breakfast and a dip in the pool. (Since this is about the only place in town to stay, advance reservations might be prudent.) Across the street is a fine cafe with good cooking and even better service.

From Monticello continue north on 191 for about 12 miles, where you turn left (west) onto State Highway 211. This is the road to *Canyonlands National Park.* As your map indicates, you are still a good 30 miles or more from the actual

On a pristine fall morning, a travel agent from California scales the sandstone bluffs of Big Spring Canyon Overlook at Canyonlands National Park, Utah. Photograph by George F. Thompson.

national park entrance, so enjoy the sights and sounds along the way. A "must" stop is the *Newspaper Rock State Park* on your right, which features more than 350 petroglyphs crammed together on a smooth rockface. After getting your fill of these petroglyphs and the arts and crafts that are for sale at this site, continue west and take note of the beautiful scenery along *Indian Creek* and the canyons one can see off to both sides of the highway. Most travelers at this point realize that this area is, indeed, something special and their entire being begins to come to rest and to entertain the thought of reaching a higher spiritual plane. One is quite surprised to remember that one is still outside the national park boundary.

The immediate destination is the *Needles Visitor Center* (4,960 feet) just inside the park boundary. Here one will want to take advantage of the rest rooms and the advice the park rangers will give you on what to do and see given your time limitations. The park is always open, but the visitor center is open from 0800 until 1630 on Monday through Friday. There is an admission fee. (For more information, contact the Superintendent, Canyonlands National Park, 125 West 200 South, Moab, Utah 84512, U.S.A. or telephone 801-259-7164.)

Canyonlands National Park totals 337,570 acres. When the great explorer John Wesley Powell first navigated the *Green* and *Colorado rivers* in 1869 and 1871 (the two rivers join in the park), he had this to say about the place: "Wherever we look there is but a wilderness of rocks; deep gorges where the rivers are lost below cliffs and towers and pinnacles; and ten thousand strangely carved forms in every direction; and beyond them, mountains blending with the clouds."

This was also Indian country. The Fremont and Anasazi peoples hunted and farmed along the rivers from about AD 1000 to 1250, and ruins of Anasazi pueblos and granaries can be found at *Salt Creek*. Anglo trappers arrived as early as 1836, and by the 1870s ranchers grazed their cattle along the rivers. The canyonlands were also used as natural hideouts for rustlers and outlaws, including the famous Butch Cassidy and his Wild Bunch.

One of the great Americans of the twentieth century is Stewart Udall, who was secretary of the interior under Presidents John F. Kennedy and Lyndon Baynes Johnson. Canyonlands became a national park in 1964 as a result of his efforts, and many Americans today from both political

Visitors are encouraged to get out of their vehicle and into the landscape to explore the unique environments at Arches National Park, Utah. Photographs by George F. Thompson.

parties wish there were more public leaders of his kind in the higher echelons of power.

One must, reluctantly, leave Canyonlands, even if the extent of one's visit is to travel down the paved highway until it dead-ends at *Big Spring Canyon Overlook* (4,880 feet). On one of our recent outings with the New Mexico Geographical Society, it seemed that every one of our nineteen passengers shared the same two feelings: First, that they would return soon and spend as much time as possible and, second, that this park should never be threatened with development or by unappreciative tourists.

For those who can spend two days away from the regular *Beyond the Great Divide* route, continue north (left) at the junction of State Highway 211 and U.S. Highway 191. In about 84 miles U.S. Highway 191 enters *Moab,* Utah (4,000 feet), a popular tourist stop for river rafting on the Colorado River and excursions into *Arches National Park,* which is a little over 5 miles beyond Moab on 191. Arches became a national monument in 1929 and, after several major additions, a national park in 1971. It currently contains 73,379 acres and the largest number of stone arches in the United States. Arches is more accessible by car than is Canyonlands and, as a result, it is much more frequented by tourist traffic. The visitor center is open daily from 0800 until 1800 during mid-March through mid-October; it is open daily from 0800 until 1640 during mid-October through mid-March. (For more information, contact the Superintendent, Arches National Park, P.O. Box 907, Moab, Utah 84532, U.S.A. or telephone 801-259-8161.)

After you experience Arches, leave enough time (two hours is best) to travel one of the most spectacular drives in the United States: State Highway 128 along the Colorado River. Turn left after leaving Arches and head toward Moab on U.S. Highway 191. Immediately after crossing the Colorado River, turn left onto *State Highway 128.* Travel as far north as the abandoned Texaco Station on your right, then turn around and follow 128 back toward Moab. And get your cameras ready, for this scenery is photogenic, though, for some reason, not worthy of national park status!

To return to the *Beyond the Great Divide* route, simply follow U.S. Highway 191 back to Monticello and farther south to Bluff (a total of about 131 miles).

Our first 10 miles of travel beyond Bluff is along the *San Juan Valley* with its band of cottonwoods, then through stepped plateaus with lovely pastel shades of rock to deep red sandstones, across dry *arroyos* (small streams, creeks, or rivulets), past some small badlands, across barren sandstones, over scenic sweeps of desert shrub and grass. Here and there are a few cows.

At 11 miles west of Bluff we crest a ridge. Ahead are the impressive landforms of *Monument Valley*—bold in outline, magnificent in color. We move onward 9.5 miles amidst this exotic landscape to the turnoff to *Goosenecks State Park*. Follow this turnoff (State Highway 261 north) for almost a mile, then turn left (State Highway 316) and proceed 3.7 miles farther to the Goosenecks overlook (4,970 feet). The *San Juan River* is about 1,000 feet below, flowing through incised meanders. This stream was once flowing on a nearly level alluvial plain, but as the Colorado Plateau was slowly uplifted, the downward cutting of the San Juan River maintained its old meanders. (Note: Meander is the ancient name of the Menderes River, located about 210 miles south of Istanbul, Turkey; that stream is the classic example of river course entrenchment with change of base-level.) Vegetation in this locale (average annual precipitation is only 6.3 inches) includes yucca, saltbush (an aggressive exotic), sand sage, and Indian ricegrass. Animals roundabout are the jackrabbit, desert rodents, coyote, bobcat, gray fox, and skunk.

Return to U.S. Highway 163, turn right, and follow 163 for 3 miles through Mexican Hat, then onward past Goulding's Trading Post, and on to Kayenta.

The "Great Gooseneck" meanders of the San Juan River, near Mexican Hat, Utah, offers the traveler one of the more impressive sites in the Interior West. Photograph by Cotton Mather.

The small settlement of *Mexican Hat* gets its name from a huge boulder, 60 feet wide and 12 feet thick, perched on a 200-foot cliff. River trips on the San Juan, a tributary of the Colorado River, are available here. The river at Mexican Hat was a barrier until a bridge was constructed in 1909. Few people lodge or eat at Mexican Hat, but it is possible.

The 53-mile trip from Mexican Hat to Kayenta passes through the heart of *Monument Valley.* This is a land of dramatic spires, sand dunes, pre-Columbian cliff dwellings, volcanic necks, igneous dikes, block mesas, slender buttes, and few people. Along our way is *Goulding's Trading Post,* opened in 1923 by Harry and Mike Goulding. Harry persuaded Hollywood film director John Ford (b. 1895; d. 1973) to visit this area. The film *Stagecoach*

Monument Valley, a part of the Colorado Plateau near the Arizona-Utah boundary, has appeared in countless Hollywood westerns and Madison Avenue car commercials and advertisements. Photograph by Cotton Mather.

(1939), which starred John Wayne (b. 1907; d. 1979), was the first major public introduction to the natural splendor of Monument Valley. Today, visitors reach backland areas by guided jeep trips and horseback tours, arranged at the nearby Monument Valley Navajo Tribal Park or at Goulding's. Good lodging, a fine panoramic view, and meals are available at Goulding's. Reservations are needed most of the year (telephone 801-727-3231 or write P.O. Box 1, Monument Valley, Utah 84536, U.S.A.).

Beyond Mexican Hat, 7.5 miles on the right, is the *Alhambra,* an igneous dike sculptured by erosion into many slender columns.

Just over the Arizona state line is *Monument Pass* (5,209 feet), so named because of natural monuments that closely border the highway.

The long, northeast-southwest trending *Comb Ridge,* on our left, is the steeply inclined sedimentary rock of the faulted Comb Monocline. *Agatha Peak* (7,100 feet), a few miles north of Kayenta and on our left, is a volcanic (Tertiary) neck. Three others are nearby. The volcanoes associated with them are now eroded away.

We arrive at *Kayenta* (5,798 feet), advisedly with lodging reservations! This desert outpost was established in 1910 as a trading post. Fifty years ago it had a population of twenty. Now it is bursting in the summer and fall with more visitors than accommodations.

Kayenta, Arizona, to Grand Canyon National Park, Arizona

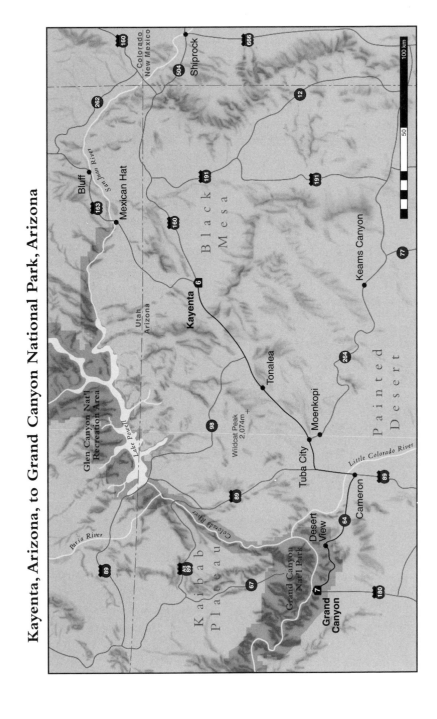

△ Day Six

KAYENTA, ARIZONA, TO GRAND CANYON NATIONAL PARK, ARIZONA, 163 MILES

Our sixth day will be a morning drive over the Colorado Plateau to the Grand Canyon, mostly through Navajo and Hopi territory. After lunch at the Grand Canyon, we shall have the entire afternoon there to explore.

Kayenta, Arizona, to Tuba City, Arizona, 72 miles, Highway 160

Kayenta, at the junction of U.S. Highways 160 and 163, has a population of 3,460 and it is booming. It is the largest town within 75 miles and is reportedly the most amorphous urban glob in the Interior West. After seeing Kayenta, it is easy to comprehend why there is no other town near it. Yet Kayenta does have gas stations, a few motels, and two or three places where you can get a Navajo taco. If you really want to slow down, try the mélange of gastronomic challenges they pile on thick, gooey, greasy fry-bread. They claim that it separates the men from the boys. In any event, it will ease your food budget for days.

From Kayenta, take U.S. Highway 160 southwest for 84 miles to the junction with U.S. Highway 89, which is 12 miles beyond Tuba City. This colorful section crosses Mesozoic sedimentary rocks 63 million to 240 million years of age. Most of the area is desert, though higher portions have piñon and juniper.

Beyond Kayenta is *Marsh Pass* (6,700 feet), an outcrop of red and brown sandstone. Shortly thereafter is the paved Arizona Highway 564 on the right, which leads 9 miles north to the *Navajo National Monument* headquarters (7,286 feet). The headquarters has museum exhibits on the Anasazi Indians, particularly the Kayenta Anasazi, whose principal home the Monument preserves and who are recognized as the premier potters of the Anasazi. A visit to the museum requires no advance planning. There is also free camping plus picnic grounds that are open from mid-April until mid-October. Nearby are the *Betatakin* ruins and *Keet Seel* ruins. Betatakin ("ledge house" in Navajo) comprises 135 connected rooms that are tucked into the cliffside. Keet Seel, the largest cliff dwelling in Arizona and one of the best preserved, has 155 rooms and six kivas. To visit the ruins, visitors must take a guided tour with a park ranger on a 2.5-mile trail that drops 700 feet. One must allow several hours for such a hike. (For information, telephone 602-672-2366 or 602-672-2367.) Return to U.S. Highway 160 and proceed south to Tonalea, 18 miles ahead.

Tonalea (6,457 feet), a Navajo word meaning "where water sinks in," is 50 miles southwest of Kayenta and has a population of 162. Just before Tonalea, on the right, note *Elephant Legs*— huge sandstone columns suggesting the feet and legs of an elephant.

Upon departure from Tonalea, observe on the right *Wildcat Peak* (6,648 feet) and *White Mesa*. Wildcat Peak is a volcanic neck with associated dikes. White Mesa is sandstone capped with white rock and edged into numerous box canyons.

Black Mesa is a low feature to the east of Tonalea where coal is strip-mined, with royalties going to the Navajo and Hopi Indians.

Our traverse from Kayenta to the Grand Canyon National Park is through the northwest portion of the *Navajo Reservation*. This reservation, about the size of West Virginia or South Carolina, completely surrounds the *Hopi Reservation*. The Hopis, a peaceful Pueblo group, occupied this territory long before the ingress of the

Navajo. The Hopi were an agricultural people, while the Navajo were hunters and gatherers until the advent of the Spanish.

The Navajo on occasion raided the Hopi settlements; this did little to foster friendship. From the Spanish, the Navajo acquired horses, goats, sheep, and cattle. Livestock numbers on communally controlled land expanded inordinately. Overgrazing and erosion ensued. (Pray that you don't run into one of the infamous Navajo-induced duststorms, which can be vicious. In the spring of 1991, particulate from such a duststorm reached as far east as Signal Mountain, Tennessee!) To add to the irony, the Navajo Reservation is loaded with coal, uranium, and petroleum (not to forget roadside litter). Today there is conflict between the Navajo and the Hopi over grazing territory, plus controversy concerning water and mineral rights. In addition, the Navajo are deeply split among themselves; the traditionalists (long may they live and prosper) wish to preserve their environment, but the quick-money enthusiasts favor scarring the land with hideous open-pit coal mines that supply the electrical generation plants (heavy air polluters, as no doubt you have noticed) with coal. Not all Indians are the pure environmentalists most of us believe them to be. For some, this must be the equivalent of learning, as a child, that there is no Santa Claus.

Continue south on U.S. Highway 160 until you reach Tuba City at the junction of Arizona Highway 264. *Tuba City* (4,550 feet) has a population of 5,045. It was named after Tuve, a Hopi leader. The settlement was established, however, by Erastus Snow, a Mormon missionary, but the Mormons were compelled to sell to the federal government when the Navajo Reservation was enlarged. Fifty years ago, Tuba City had only 124 people. Now it is a bustling trade center with an Indian hospital and modern grocery stores. (This is an excellent location to replenish travelers' coolers and to buy delicatessen sandwiches—and a bale of hay for your horse— for a picnic lunch outdoors. At the junction of 264 and 160, turn right and then to the left at the big grocery store in the shopping center.)

Moenkopi, a Hopi settlement of about 1,200 people, is 1 mile east of Tuba City on *Moenkopi Wash.* A bluff, just beyond the town

Hay is for sale at the Van Trading Company in Tuba City, Arizona. Navajo buy groceries here and hay for their horses. Photograph by Cotton Mather.

itself on Arizona State Highway 264, affords a fine view of the irrigated fields of corn and squash along the Moenkopi Wash. One almost feels as if one is going back in time when one looks down on such a landscape. Return to Tuba City on 264 West.

Tuba City, Arizona, to Grand Canyon National Park, Arizona, 93 miles, Highways 160, 89, and 64

Our route on U.S. Highway 160 continues west of Tuba City for 12 miles, then left (south) for 17 miles on U.S. Highway 89 (just 2 short miles beyond *Cameron*) to the junction with Arizona Highway 64. This trek on 89 to Cameron crosses the *Painted Desert,* a

SIDE TRIP TO HOPI CULTURAL CENTER, MCGEE AND HUBBELL TRADING POSTS, AND PETRIFIED FOREST NATIONAL PARK

No matter where *Beyond the Great Divide* takes the traveler, it seems there is always something else to see and visit just off the tour's main route. For a great, full one-day side trip, take Arizona Highway 264 to the east from *Tuba City* (past Moenkopi) all the way through the Hopi Reservation to the Navajo capital at *Window Rock,* on the Arizona-New Mexico border—a distance of 155 "non-interstate" miles. But if you want to enhance your journey even more, then plan to make this a great, full two-day side trip so that you can visit the remarkable Petrified Forest National Park and the magnificent McGees Gallery in Holbrook.

The trip from Tuba City to Window Rock is through one of the most sparsely settled areas in the United States, but it is scenic and filled with historic and contemporary aspects of Hopi and Navajo culture. Highlights include several ancient and contemporary Hopi settlements, including the Hopi Cultural Center at Second Mesa (62 miles east of Tuba City); McGee and Son's Trading Post at Keams Canyon (19 miles east of Second Mesa); and the Hubbell Trading Post National Historic Site in Ganado (74 miles east of Keams Canyon).

The only suitable lodging en route (though one can also stay at the Navajo Nation Inn and Dining Room in Window Rock) is at the *Hopi Cultural Center,* where you can obtain Hopi food and lodging in a pueblo-style complex. You will long remember with satisfaction an overnight stay here (especially if you let the hostess at the restaurant seat you with a menu and if you try something other than Hopi lamb stew), but reservations are a necessity (telephone 602-734-6650).

At the center one can visit a small museum and peruse the few shops in which one will find Hopi jewelry and other wares. Hopi pottery can be found at *First Mesa,* a few miles to the east on State Highway 264. The most traditional of the Hopi pots will be the red ones. As you did at Santa Clara and San Ildefonso Pueblos, look for "pottery for sale" signs along the highway and in the village itself (both below the mesa and on top of the mesa). Buses and wide vehicles cannot reach the top of the mesa, where the road is narrow and dangerous; cars have to be proceed slowly and cautiously, but can make it.

The *McGee and Son's Trading Post* (telephone 602-738-2295) is 19 miles east of Second Mesa at Keam's Canyon. This is one of the finest and longest established trading posts in the Southwest. For years it was operated by Cliff and Bill McGee; now it is under the management of Ron and Bruce, who are Cliff's sons. Their major present trading post (McGees Gallery), however, is 68 miles to the south at Holbrook. We visit Holbrook on the second day of this side trip.

East of Keam's Canyon 42 miles, in Ganado, is the *Hubbell Trading Post* (telephone 602-755-3475), a national historic site under the direction of the National Park Service since 1967. Founded in 1878 by John Lorenzo Hubbell (b. 1853; d. 1930), an honest trader and an enthusiastic promoter of Navajo crafts, it is the oldest continually active Navajo trading post. It is operated on much the same system as in early years in the merchandising of jewelry, rugs, groceries, dry goods, and horse gear. Bill Malone, who operated the old trading post at *Piñon* (northeast of Second Mesa) from 1962 to 1981, is the manager. Bill is a genial and extraordinarily competent person who worked for the McGee family for two decades. He is married to a Navajo woman and has five handsome children. He speaks the Navajo language and is steeped in Indian culture. Veteran rug dealers regard the

Hubbell Trading Post and McGee's two posts (at Keam's Canyon and Holbrook) as perhaps the prime places in the United States for acquiring hand-loomed Navajo rugs.

Continue east of Ganado on State Highway 264 until you reach *Window Rock*. As you approach the town, turn left at the sign that says "Fort Defiance," and then follow the signs for the tribal center. Window Rock (6,764 feet), population 2,363, is named after a natural sandstone arch and it became the tribal capital of the Navajo Nation in the early 1930s. As you drive into the capital grounds to see the arch, you pass governmental building after governmental building, which exemplify the full flowering of bureaucratic development among the Navajo. At Window Rock, visit the *Navajo Arts and Crafts Center.* Tourist accommodations are available at the *Navajo Nation Inn and Dining Room* (telephone 602-871-4108).

The Navajo language was used effectively in World War II to transmit American battle plans; Japanese intelligence officers were unable to decode the messages. It is claimed that even Navajo children can decipher these transmittals.

If you have only one day to spare, then return to Tuba City directly to the west on State Highway 264. If you have a second day, then return west on 264 for only a short distance to the town of *St. Michaels,* where you turn left (south) on the only road. You are heading for *Lupton* and Interstate Highway 40, about 20 miles away.

Proceed on I-40 to the west for approximately 47 miles, where you take the exit for the *Petrified Forest National Park* and *Painted Desert.* You will want to stop at the *Painted Desert Visitor Center* to take advantage of the rest rooms and information one can obtain on the park. At the visitor center, for example, one can view a seventeen-minute film on how wood is petrified. At the south end of the park, one can visit the *Rainbow Forest Museum,* which has exhibits of petrified woods (in case you don't get your fill outside) and of the

Visitors from Ohio and New Mexico record their visit to Petrified Forest National Park with "sure-shot" cameras. Petroglyphs are visible in the foreground. Photograph by George F. Thompson.

area's geological and human past. The drive from the north end to the south end is 27 miles, and there are frequent pullouts. Although the main attraction of the park is the forest of petrified wood (some 225 million years old), there are also prehistoric ruins and petroglyphs to see. (Note: Obey the park's commandment—do not take with you any petrified wood, no matter how small. Outside the park, in convenience and souvenir stores and especially in the town of *St. Johns,* Arizona, one can easily find petrified wood for sale.) Anyone who is planning a long hike or wilderness camping should tell park rangers of your plans and have appropriate gear and provisions (such as plenty of water and sun screen). The park is open daily from 0600 to 1900 from June through August and from 0800 to 1700 from September through May. There is an admission fee. (For information, contact the Superintendent, Painted Desert Visitor Center, Petrified Forest National Park, Arizona 86028, U.S.A. or telephone 602-524-6228.)

As you depart the park and are immediately inundated with signs that say "Petrified Wood 4 Sale," turn right on U.S. Highway 180 and head for *Holbrook* (5,075 feet), 20 miles to the northwest. At the junction of 180 and State Highway 77, turn right and head into town. You will cross the railroad tracks, pass through the stoplight, stay straight on Main Street and go under the interstate bridge, and then, in a little over .5 mile, turn right into *McGees Gallery* (telephone 602-524-1977), one of the premiere places in the Southwest to view and purchase traditional and more contemporary Indian rugs, jewelry, pots, sand paintings, and other Indian crafts. Bruce McGee is in charge of this gallery, which is the latest and most modern of the three McGee trading posts. Bruce is one of the most accomplished, knowledgeable, and respected traders in all Indian country, and he will take great pleasure in explaining the difference between "traditional" Indian rugs, jewelry, pots, sand paintings, and other crafts and those that are "beyond native tradition."

The McGee family is one of the oldest and most esteemed trading post families in the Southwest, and the history of the McGee trading posts, to a remarkable degree, represents the history of all the trading posts in Indian country. In the days before the automobile and four-wheel-drive truck, the trading posts were located where the Indians were—in remote, interior areas, far removed from the travel lanes of whites. They were accessible only on horseback or by horse-drawn vehicles. With the development of U.S. Highway 66, however, came the advent of modern tourism in the Southwest, and so Indians began to sell some of their goods along the highway. Rugs were hung over posts and often sold simply by the pound!

As a consequence of this initial movement away from the isolated Indian homeland toward the more visited highways, some trading post operators, seeing the light of tourist dollars, moved their trading posts to Route 66 or to minor unpaved highways, which later were to be paved. This progressive movement of following improvements in transportation corridors (i.e., roads and highways) has continued to the present, so that today almost all trading post locations are on good highway locations, and many of them that were on the minor highways have relocated along the transcontinental interstate. (It was also during this time that the Indians relinquished the horse as the primary mode of transportation, opting instead for the mobility and comfort and expense of the pick-up truck.)

The McGee trading posts clearly reflect this movement from remote location to better highway location to interstate location. For decades Bruce and Ron McGee's father and uncle operated a fine trading post (still renowned) at *Piñon* in the isolated backcountry northeast of Second Mesa. The road into Piñon was dirt, rough, and ungraded, and an old-time dealer such as Cotton Mather really had to want to carry fine Indian rugs, pots, and jewelry in his gallery to make such a journey worth the effort. This was the old West! (Note: The road to Piñon was paved only in the late 1950s, and then only from the main highway access to the east. The road remains unpaved today from the west.)

The McGees anticipated the changing nature of the trade, and opened their next trading post on State Highway 264, at *Keam's Canyon,* to get within better reach of their new customers—the dealers and tourists. In essence, the trading posts were trying to meet their customers halfway. A location such as McGees at Keam's Canyon was downright convenient, or at least for a while, until U.S. Highway 66 and its eventual replacement (Interstate 40) pushed customer traffic even farther to the south and away from old reliable roads such as State Highway 264. Although McGee and Son's Trading Post at Keam's Canyon is still operating and does a good business, it has become secondary to the major outlet at Holbrook along the interstate. McGees Gallery, in whose parking lot you now sit, is, then, the third-generation trading post of the McGee family. It is located just off the main Holbrook exit on Interstate 40, and this particular exit, not coincidentally, is one of the most popular overnight stopping places along I-40 in the entire state!

So as you enter McGees Gallery in Holbrook, or McGee and Son's Trading Post at Keam's Canyon, or the original trading post at Piñon, remember the history of how trading posts developed and evolved. The traders were largely responsible for creating many of the Indians arts and crafts we honor and value today, and they helped to spread the word world-wide about the unique artistry of hand-loomed rugs, and Pueblo pots, and the like. The significance of the trading posts, of the traders, and the old-time dealers cannot be underestimated in the development of the American Southwest as a distinct culture region that everyone now raves about and wants to visit.

There are two other changes in the trading post business that are worth mentioning, to complete the historical sermon. As you may have noticed, the subtitle of the McGees Gallery sign says "Beyond Native Tradition." Traders such as Bruce McGee and all the way back to Lorenzo Hubbell and like kind have encouraged and commissioned the development of new ways for Indian artists to make their rugs, pots, sand paintings, and jewelry, creating, in a way, new traditions. But the interstate also brings a new clientele to the trading posts that appreciates the new look of Indian crafts as well as the traditional forms of artistry.

The other change worth noting is the way the traders pay the Indian artists. In the old days (though one can still see this system operate at the Hubbell Trading Post National Historic Site in Ganado), the Indians would trade their rugs, pots, jewelry, and the like for all the necessities of Indian life on the reservation—groceries, hardware items, horse gear, clothing, and, ironically, factory-made blankets from the East. Accounts were kept in a ledger book, and any differential was paid in silver, not paper currency. This was the case at Piñon and Keam's Canyon for years. Now, the exchange of rugs, pots, sand paintings, jewelry, and the like is a simple cash transaction: An Indian artist brings in the goods and is paid in U.S. currency. This can be seen at Holbrook.

Oh, by the way, be sure to tell Bruce and Ron McGee and Bill Malone that Cotton Mather sends his best regards. And no visit to Holbrook is complete without eating lunch or dinner at *Romo's Cafe* downtown, just a block off Main Street. Here one can enjoy excellent Mexican cuisine at very reasonable prices.

From Holbrook, return east on Interstate 40 for about 4 miles. Then take State Highway 77 north for about 55 scenic miles, where you will rejoin State Highway 264. Turn left (west) on 264, and follow it past Keam's Canyon, past First and Second Mesa, past Moenkopi, before reuniting with *Beyond the Great Divide* at Tuba City.

broad floodplain in Triassic time of 205 million to 240 million years ago. The Painted Desert material is soft, barely consolidated silt and volcanic ash that erodes readily. The ash has been altered into bentonite, a clay that swells when wet and cracks when dry and is too loose for plants to readily anchor their roots.

Cameron (4,200 feet), with an estimated population of 800, has a trading post, a restaurant, and a post office that was established in 1917. Cameron is located at a bridge over the *Little Colorado River.* The first bridge here was built in 1911.

A Navajo hogan (pronounced ho-gan, not ho-gun), west of Window Rock, Arizona. Photograph by Cotton Mather.

About 2 miles south of Cameron, turn right (west) on Arizona Highway 64 and proceed 56 miles to Grand Canyon Village on the South Rim. As we head west, we ascend the great monocline that is the eastern edge of the *Kaibab Plateau*. The surface formation, the Kaibab Limestone, is at about 7,000 feet elevation south of the Grand Canyon and 8,200 feet elevation north of the canyon. At *Desert View Point,* 34 miles west of Cameron, the elevation is 7,438 feet; 24 miles to the west, at Grand Canyon Village, the elevation is 6,850 feet.

The *Grand Canyon* of the *Colorado River* is one of the three most spectacular sights in the world. Nowhere else can one look so far back into history, two billion years back! The *Inner Gorge,* visible along the *South Rim* on our route, has exposed rock of the late Precambrian era. Overlying this rock, which is the Vishnu

The Grand Canyon of the Colorado River, one of nature's miracles, is an extremely popular destination for foreign travelers. Photograph by Cotton Mather.

Schist, is the sedimentary rocks formed during subsequent millions of years. About one billion years ago, this region was uplifted and tilted so the Inner Gorge formations are now gently inclined. After the uplift, erosion removed perhaps a half billion years of the lithologic period. Subsequently, numerous depositional and erosional cycles occurred, during which there were great climatic, vegetative, and animal life changes. Today, we find a great ecological range in the canyon and the region. The bottom of the canyon is at 2,400 feet and the top of the San Francisco Peaks is at 12,633 feet. The San Francisco Peaks are 90 miles to the southeast (northeast of Flagstaff, elevation 6,899 feet). Within this range of about 10,000 vertical feet is a life contrast equivalent to that between northern Mexico and southern Canada. Isn't nature something?

The temperatures are hot in summer at the bottom of the canyon. Indeed, they are 20 degrees Fahrenheit warmer on average than on the South Rim. Seasonal ranges are pronounced. *Bright Angel Ranger Station,* for example, has an average of 21 degrees Fahrenheit in January while the average in July is 62 degrees Fahrenheit. Average annual precipitation is 26.9 inches, three times greater than at Kayenta. In winter, snowfall is heavy.

Three great overlooks in *Grand Canyon Village* are at *Grandeur, Yavapai,* and *Mather Points.* At these places one views not only the spectacular cleft that exposes so much geological history, but also the *Colorado River* that is a vertical mile below the rim. The so-called mighty Mississippi River descends only 1,000 feet from its source in northern Minnesota to the Gulf of Mexico in Louisiana, while the Colorado River's waters fall more than twelve times that vertical distance on its surge from its source in Rocky Mountain National Park (northeastern Grand County) to the Gulf of California in Mexico. "Colorado" is the Spanish word for "colored" (especially red), and it is highly colored by reddish sediment as it roars through this canyon. Artists fall into a trance, approaching sheer delirium, as they absorb the spectacle of the colorful Colorado River and the chromatic tones of the canyon walls; tourists armed with "sure shot" cameras and loads of color film do, too. All of this is immensely enhanced by the intricately sculptured rock forms of the canyon walls whose images are transformed through the daylight hours and are so lovely in the mist of midnight moonlight. Thomas Moran (b. 1837; d. 1926), the great landscape painter, certainly portrayed it; now you can see it!

Who first gazed upon the Grand Canyon? Archeologists have evidence of human habitation there dating to at least 2000 BC. Later were the Anasazi who came at approximately AD 500, but they abandoned the Grand Canyon about AD 1150 because of prolonged drought. Later immigrants were ancestors of the Hualapai and Havasupai who still dwell in the western part of the canyon.

The first white explorer to float down the Grand Canyon and leave a good account of the expedition was Major John Wesley Powell (b. 1834; d. 1902) in 1869, whose exploits we described earlier in the book. Now thousands have made the journey and the

The El Tovar Hotel, at the South Rim of the Grand Canyon, was completed in 1905. Photograph by Cotton Mather.

river is so overloaded with rafters that the National Park Service regulates the number.

The South Rim is officially open all year, though winter snows can be a problem. (For winter road conditions, telephone 602-638-2245.) The *Visitor Center,* 1 mile east of Grand Canyon Village, has a museum and an information service. Trips by muleback can be arranged from both the South and North rims. Some people take the trail and stay overnight at Phantom Ranch at the bottom of the canyon. Advance reservations are necessary (telephone 602-638-2401). But the trip is strenuous. Some people prefer hiking rather than having a sore derrière from riding muleback. Overnight hikers are obliged to obtain a camping permit. For information on the various trails, consult the officials at the Visitor Center.

Grand Canyon Village (6,850 feet) is a complex on the South Rim that includes the El Tovar Hotel, the Hopi House, Verkamp's

Curios, Babbitt's General Store, and Bright Angel Lodge. The *El Tovar Hotel* was completed in 1905 by Hopi craftsmen at a cost of $250,000. Logs for the building were shipped by railroad from Oregon; the stone is native Kaibab Limestone. The hotel is operated by the National Parks Division of Fred Harvey, Inc. *Phantom Ranch,* the hostel at the bottom of the canyon at Bright Angel Creek, was constructed in 1922. *Bright Angel Lodge* was built in 1935.

Today, Grand Canyon National Park is literally under siege. Photography is impaired by polluted air, reportedly from the Four Corners Power Plant 20 miles east of Shiprock in New Mexico. Acid rain threatens the vegetation. The auditory blast from helicopters and airplanes in and over the canyon is distressing. All public facilities are jammed in summer and fall. To worsen conditions, the budget of the National Park Service has been slashed since President Jimmy Carter left office in 1980. President Theodore Roosevelt (b. 1858; d. 1919), in a 1903 speech, stated that the Grand Canyon was "the most impressive piece of scenery I have ever looked at." Teddy Roosevelt did much as President to advance the cause of conservation in the United States. Were he alive today, one wonders what would he declare upon a return visit to the Grand Canyon. Certainly more than "Bully!"

The National Park System of the United States remains a model for countries around the world, and its rangers are as dedicated a bunch of employees as an employer could ever want. But problems do persist, especially at the "crown jewels" such as the Grand Canyon, Yellowstone in Wyoming, and Yosemite in California. When the first national parks were established, they were isolated to the American public and difficult and expensive to get to. But now the Park Service is battling a dilemma known as "loving the parks to death." There are no easy solutions in the conflict between conserving the resource and opening up the parks to every kind of visitor imaginable, but certainly policies of park management will have to change to meet the contemporary challenge. Many fine books on the national parks exist, but two of the finest are *Steve Mather of the National Parks,* by Robert Shankland (1951, 1954, 1970), and *Mountains Without Handrails: Reflections on the Na-*

tional Parks, by Joseph L. Sax (1980). Also, everyone should own a copy of *Bravo 20: The Bombing of the American West,* by Richard Misrach with Myriam Weisang Misrach (1990), one of the most important books to be published in decades, whose proposal for a new kind of national park is remarkable.

△ *Day Seven*

GRAND CANYON NATIONAL PARK, ARIZONA, TO KINGMAN, ARIZONA, 188 MILES

Our agenda of our final day is to go south from Grand Canyon Village on Arizona Highway 64 to Williams and then westward on Interstate Highway 40 (I-40), parallel to the renowned old U.S. Highway 66. All of this is over the Colorado Plateau until the last few miles when we descend the western escarpment into Kingman for lunch.

Grand Canyon Village, Arizona, to Williams, Arizona, 58 miles, Highway 64

Travel to the Grand Canyon before 1901 was a rare and rib-rattling experience. The only transportation available was stagecoach over rough wagon roads, 58 miles from Williams or 77 miles from Flagstaff. From either town, it was a bruising, dirty, all-day expedition.

The *Santa Fe Railroad* completed a line from Williams to the South Rim in 1901, and train service with steam locomotive power was then initiated. By 1905, you could luxuriate in the sumptuous setting of the El Tovar Hotel where Fred Harvey was a concessionaire. At Williams you could stay at the Fray Marcos Hotel, and be served by one of the Harvey girls to a full-course dinner for $1.50. Fred Harvey (b. 1835; d. 1901), an Englishman, perturbed by bad food in the Southwest, proposed a plan to the Santa Fe Railroad in

Grand Canyon National Park, Arizona, to Kingman, Arizona

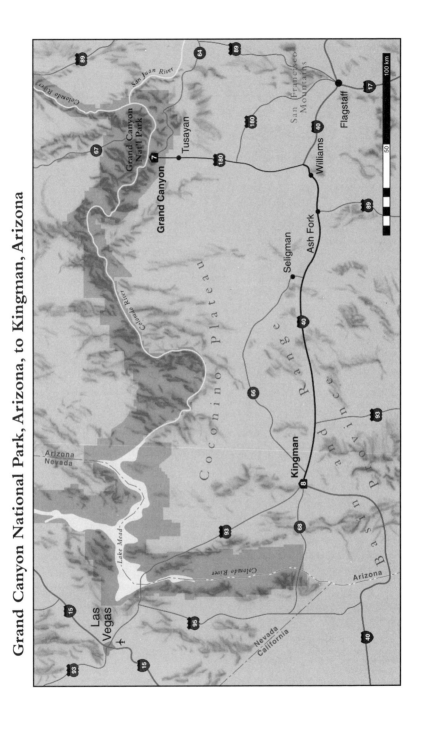

the 1870s for Spanish-style decor, digestible food, and good service. The Santa Fe Railroad accepted the plan and, by the end of the nineteenth century, there were Harvey Houses at 100-mile intervals throughout much of the region. Harvey hired in the East eighteen- to thirty-year-old women of wholesome character, and that ended the adage of "no ladies west of Dodge City and no women west of Albuquerque." The women received $17.50 a month and were obliged to live in dormitories supervised by a housemother. The waitresses were expertly trained, the table settings were attractive, and men were not served unless they wore a coat. Fred Harvey became famous. What the United States of America needs today is not a good five-cent cigar, but rather a good five-cent buffalo nickel and a reincarnation of Fred Harvey and his Harvey girls!

Leaving Grand Canyon Village, from *Mather Point,* south on Arizona Highway 64 (also U.S. Highway 180), it is 5.8 miles to *Tusayan* (6,540 feet), population about 260 with ambitions for 2,600. Founded in 1934, Tusayan is, at this writing, a typically American mishmash of motels, restaurants, sandwich shops, trading post, food mart, gas stations, helicopter bases for Grand Canyon flights, movie theater, car rental agencies, and campground for "recreational vehicles." This scene again reflects an apparent propensity on the part of city officials in the United States to avoid even modest environmental design and planning schemes that would help alleviate this "trashing of the public landscape." Anyone needing a refresher course on this scenic blight should read (or reread) Peter Blake's classic book, *God's Own Junkyard* (1964). It is a shame that one's last memory of the Grand Canyon, coming out of the South Rim and Mather Point, is of Tusayan, or at least Tusayan as it is today.

South of Tusayan 22 miles is the junction of U.S. Highway 180 and State Highway 64. Two motels, a gas station, a store, and a privately owned campground are at this junction. We continue southward on Arizona Highway 64.

On the east side of the road, 5.7 miles farther south, is an artificial pond. The woven wire fencing on both sides of the road is for sheep (linear wire is for cattle). Water is a big problem here.

In winter, sheep and horses will eat snow to fulfill their water requirements, but cattle will not. Notwithstanding, there are some cattle in this locale.

Water is trucked from Williams to the lodges on the South Rim of the Grand Canyon. The lodges pump some water from the Colorado River, but they are plagued by leaky penstocks. High food prices at the South Rim are partially attributed to the problem of water.

Our travel to Williams is through a fine tall forest, piñon pine and juniper, and steppe grass. The change in vegetation is a response to variations in elevation and soil. Most of our travel to Williams is over the Kaibab Limestone, though the latter portion traverses lava flows and terrain with well-rounded cinder cones. About 35 miles to the east of our highway is *San Francisco Mountain,* also referred to as San Francisco Peaks. This is a volcano that collapsed on the northeast side into a magma chamber. Erosion by Pleistocene glaciers left the volcano with three peaks, one of which is *Humphreys Peak* (12,670 feet)—the highest elevation in Arizona.

Williams (6,762 feet), named after guide and trapper Bill Williams (b. 1787; d. 1849), was founded in 1881. The town is set in a semi-basin, partially surrounded by several low volcanic peaks. Today's population of 2,266 is about one-fourth less than it was a half century ago. In contrast, *Flagstaff* (6,899 feet), 30 miles to the east, increased in the same period from about 22,000 to 44,500. Williams has two east-west main streets: Railroad Avenue and Bill Williams Avenue. Both main streets look old; few new buildings have been constructed in the last fifty years.

Williams was once an important tourist and lumber town. I-40 has three exits into town, but not one motel is located at these exits. All of the motels in Williams are older ones built when the famous old U.S. Highway 66 ("Get your kicks on Route 66") went through the middle of town. Today's jewel in Williams is the Grand Canyon Railway depot on the north side of the tracks. From here one can now ride in comfort in authentically restored Harriman coach cars of the 1920s, pulled by a 1910 steam locomotive. The *"Williams Flyer"* departs at 0930 and returns at 1845, with nearly four hours at the Grand Canyon. (For reservations and information, telephone 800-843-8724.)

SIDE TRIP TO SAN FRANCISCO MOUNTAINS, MUSEUM OF NORTHERN ARIZONA, AND FLAGSTAFF

The main purpose of this half-day side trip is to let you experience the beautiful scenery and impressive lava flows and cones along U.S. Highway 180, which takes you to *Flagstaff* (51 miles) through the *Kaibab National Forest,* in the shadow of the volcanic *San Francisco Mountains* and *Humphrey's Peak* (12,670 feet, which is the highest point in Arizona), and through the groves of aspen (*Populus tremuloides michx.*), which are spectacular in their autumnal glory around the first week or two of October.

We have just traveled south from Grand Canyon Village and Mather Point past Tusayan, and south of Tusayan 22 miles to the junction of U.S. Highway 180 and State Highway 64. Rather than follow the prescribed tour route to Williams on 64, turn left (southeast) on 180 and simply enjoy the scenery described above. You will not be disappointed (but pray that housing developments are never allowed to enter this landscape, as they have on U.S. Highway 89 north of Flagstaff).

The *Museum of Northern Arizona* (established 1928) is 3 miles north of Flagstaff on 180. Here one can spend an hour or two among the extensive collections that emphasize the human settlement of the Colorado Plateau, from the paleo-Indians (15,000 to 8,000 BC) to the Hopi and Navajo of today. The museum is open daily from 9:00 to 17:00, except for Thanksgiving, Christmas, and New Year's Day. (For information, telephone 602-774-5211.)

Proceed on 180 to *Flagstaff* (6,899 feet; population approximately 44,500 and growing) and follow the first sign you see for Interstate 40. Take I-40 to the west and rejoin *Beyond the Great Divide* in Williams, about 30 miles away.

Most of the guidebooks we own laud lovely Flagstaff, and there is no denying that it is located in one of the most picturesque settings in the West. But here human ingenuity has not improved upon the natural scene. Instead of the "clearest air in North America," we have observed in our many visits to Flagstaff over the years a rather obvious smokescreen (with accompanying stench) that is created by the sawdust burners from the extensive lumberyards on the south side of the railroad tracks. The economic importance of the timber industry and the surrounding national forests becomes even more apparent if one visits the popular *Northern Arizona University* (established 1899). There one will observe that the newest and biggest building is for the School of Forestry.

As geographers, we are, of course, familiar with such theories as "geographies of the mind," but we still find it very difficult to get around town. Flagstaff unquestionably lacks a planned street pattern, the omnipresent railroad tracks through the center of town bring back memories of the Continental Divide, and the dispersement of new business establishments that cater to tourists is, in a word, chaotic. If you plan to spend an hour in Flagstaff before heading west for Williams, then we suggest you locate its gems—the old business district and the attractive residential section adjacent to it. Here is a glimpse not only into Flagstaff's past, but also a glimpse into what could have been its future: A town designed with nature and its natural setting in mind, rather than a post-World War II town that kowtows to the quick tourist dollar. As John Wayne is known to have said in more than one of his famous Westerns, "I call 'em as I see 'em."

Williams, Arizona, to Kingman, Arizona, 130 miles, Interstate Highway 40

From Williams to Seligman, a distance of 42 miles, we traverse a veneer of lava flows overlying Permian limestone and Triassic sandstone and shale. This is complicated by faulting and warping, and near Seligman by volcanic necks. The lava flows near Williams are less than six million years old; those between Ash Fork and Seligman are six million to fifteen million years old.

Seven miles west of Williams, our highway starts a 6 percent downgrade which continues for about 7 additional miles. The terrain for 7 miles west of Williams is vegetated with tall pine. At the bottom of the steep grade, the vegetation has changed to a combination of steppe grass and dwarf piñon pine and juniper. We shall see no more tall timber all the way to Kingman.

Ash Fork (5,144 feet) is 17 miles west of Williams. Take the byway through town. Ash Fork now has a population of about 400, a 50 percent decline in fifty years. A half century ago, U.S. Highway 66 went through the middle of town. Almost no buildings have been constructed since 1940. What you are viewing here is a museum of service stations, hotel, motels, and other business establishments of bygone days. (More than a few U.S. senators would like to see a lot of Route 66—from Chicago to Los Angeles—be restored, to became, in essence, a national historic highway, its towns included.) At the western margin of Ash Fork, however, is the enormous and very active yards of the Western Stone Company's "Kaibab Stone." Ash Fork publicizes itself as the "nation's flagstone capital." This is a sandstone shipped mainly within a radius of 750 miles. Most of it is marketed in California, from San Diego to San Francisco, and is used around swimming pools and as garden flagstone.

Seligman (5,250 feet), 25 miles west of Ash Fork, was founded in 1886 and has a population of 950, almost unchanged for the past five decades. It is another U.S. Highway 66 town with little change to mar its advertised "historic" (some might argue "hysteric") character. The only real mar is the garish Western cowboy and saloon fakery at the western margin of town.

West of Seligman, I-40 traverses Mississippian limestone—some with karst features, then lava flows, and, at approximately 44 miles west of Seligman, we cross the fault zone that marks the western edge of the *Colorado Plateau.* North of our highway, along this north-south fault zone, are the *Grand Wash Cliffs,* which are an uplift of several thousand feet along the east side of the *Grand Wash Fault.* This fault zone continues northward beyond the Arizona-Utah border, just east of the Nevada-Arizona border. And the fault zone continues southward as the *Cottonwood Cliffs,* along the *Cottonwood Fault.* Precambrian rocks are exposed along this fault.

West of the Colorado Plateau, we are in the *Basin and Range Province*—a region of low, worn-down fault-block mountains separated by basins or valleys deeply filled with detritus eroded from the mountains. The Mohave County Courthouse in Kingman is in the Basin and Range Province, approximately 30 miles west of the western edge of the Colorado Plateau. (Note: One of the newest additions to the National Park System is the Great Basin National Park near Baker, Nevada, on the Nevada-Utah border. Established in 1986, this park contains diverse natural attractions, such as Wheller Peak [13,063 feet], the Lexington Arch [a limestone formation over six stories high], a forest of bristlecone pines [*Pinus aristata*] over 3,500 years old, prehistoric rock art, and Lehman Caves [one of the nation's largest known limestone solution caverns]. Great Basin National Park is not only one of the most physically varied of our national parks, but also it is a highly instructive part of the Great Plains. Before it became a national park, it was bypassed because of its secluded location. Such neglect, in essence, kept the area intact for current visitors to appreciate and enjoy!)

Kingman (3,336 feet) was named for and by Lewis Kingman, who was the civil engineer in charge of locating and building what is now the Santa Fe Railroad. The town was founded in 1880 as a railroad camp, and was essentially established in 1882 after the rails were laid to that point in the last leg along the 35th parallel line. Kingman was important as a trade center for those people engaged in the lode mining of gold and also copper, and as an important, regular stop for early mail and passenger airlines. Its chief economic support today is—take a guess—tourism. Its population of 11,000 represents nearly a five-fold increase since World War II. Kingman is strategically located at the junction of two major highways: Interstate Highway 40 westbound leads to Los Angeles via Barstow and eastbound to every major highway system in the United States; and U.S. Highway 93 southbound leads to Phoenix and northbound to the Hoover Dam, Lake Mead Recreational Area, and Las Vegas. This creates heavy traffic and a service industry to meet the needs of tourists, truckers, and the like. Kingman has an irrigated golf course, a community college, county fairgrounds, the Methodist church where actor Clark Gable (b. 1901; d. 1960) and actress Carole Lombard (b. 1908; d. 1942) were married, and a few palm trees. These palm trees are significant: They are the first palm trees "beyond the Great Divide" and an omen that we are approaching "Southern California extended."

SOUTHERN CALIFORNIA EXTENDED

Beyond the Great Divide began in Denver, Colorado, at the western edge of the Great Plains. We have now traversed across two great regions of the United States—the Southern Rocky Mountains and the Colorado Plateau.

Kingman, Arizona, is just beyond the western edge of the Colorado Plateau, but it is only a short 70-mile jaunt to Hoover Dam, to the incredibly popular Lake Mead National Recreational Area, and to that neon delight, Las Vegas. Here in Kingman, then, is where "Beyond the Great Divide" meets "Southern California Extended." Southern California is no longer content to include only San Diego, Santa Barbara, Palm Springs, and Los Angeles. Southern California now extends far to the east, to the very western edge of the Colorado Plateau, to Las Vegas.

Here, then, is where "The Transcontinental" continues on its fourth and final leg of a great sojourn across the United States. It began with *Across the Applachians: Washington, D.C., to the Great Lakes,* proceeded with *Crossing the Heartland: Chicago to Denver,* went "beyond the Great Divide," from Denver to the Grand Canyon and Kingman, and now heads toward a final destination in Los Angeles, California—a journey that literally takes the traveler coast to coast. But for those who live in this part of the country, "Beyond the Great Divide," there is a belief that is held by many and that can be expressed in three simple words: "West is best."

But we should let poet Edwin Ford Piper have the last few words of our sojourn together. In 1924 a collection of his poems was published, and it is from this collection that we select a personal favorite, "Late Dusk," which reads as follows:

Not yet farewell. For while the shadowy creatures
Are chanting to the spirits of the dusk,
The old, loved road invites our fellowship;
I'll go apiece with you.

PART THREE

Resources

△ Hints to the Traveler

Our tour *Beyond the Great Divide*—from Denver, Colorado, on the western edge of the Great Plains, to Kingman, Arizona, on the eastern edge of Southern California Extended—is across two huge regions: the Southern Rocky Mountains and the Colorado Plateau. These are regions with great ranges of altitude and with some vast distances between cities and towns and hamlets. So the wily wanderer goes well-prepared for these conditions.

We have traveled this region regularly for over sixty years, and so we have seen great changes in the landscape. We can remember driving dirt roads to visit the old Indian trading posts, which were then far away from the present-day interstate; now, of course, they are paved two-lane and four-lane highways. We can remember sleepy little towns with few places to sleep and eat that are now major stopping-off points with plenty of motel chains and franchised eateries. We can remember a time when few people visited the Southwest, much less the Rocky Mountains.

Thus, knowing this region as well as we do, there are a few items that you might wish to consider before you actually arrive in Denver.

ACCOMMODATIONS AND PROVISIONS

The main economic base today for both the Southern Rocky Mountains and the Colorado Plateau is tourism. As a traveler, bear in mind that decent (i.e., clean and comfortable) accommodations for the tourist are often widely spaced, and that they are heavily burdened during peak vacation periods. At such times, it may be advisable to conclude the day's travel somewhat earlier than usual or to have reservations for lodging. Some locations, such as the big ski resorts during peak winter periods, may even require reservations months in advance of your scheduled arrival date.

Consider, also, taking along a cooler large enough to store your bread, luncheon meats, condiments, cheeses, fruit, fresh water, juices, soda pop, and other favorite beverages and food items. This will cut down significantly on your food budget that will remain high if you eat all your meals in restaurants, and it will allow you to partake of wayside lunches in this land of spectacular scenery. Just about everywhere on our route you will find pleasant picnic areas or safe roadside turnouts with nice views. Provisions can be replenished en route at supermarkets and at convenience stores, with one exception: If you like a cocktail hour after a long day of driving and sightseeing, be sure you don't run out of liquor, wine, or beer in Utah.

AUTOMOTIVE CONCERNS

A well-serviced and well-tuned vehicle with good tires is essential for mountain travel, so come to Denver prepared. And en route, keep a watchful eye on your fuel tank, fluids, belts, and tire pressure, for you do not want to run out of gas, deal with an overheated car, and the like, in lands as remote as this. Remember, too, that it is increasingly difficult in this part of the country, as is the case everywhere in the United States, to find an on-duty mechanic at gas stations, especially on weekends. This, of course, is for your convenience, or so the oil companies tell us.

Gasoline prices vary considerably in the West and so you may be tempted to push on (to what you think will be just) a little farther in order to save a penny or two per gallon of gas. But it is wise to keep your fuel tank at least one-third full at all times, for that next gas station (that you think is just around the corner and charges less) may, in fact, be 80 miles down the road and charge 30 cents more per gallon. Vehicles that require diesel fuel should be especially conscious of fuel consumption. It seems that every year it is harder to find diesel fuel at gas stations; it is available, but just don't press your luck.

We always carry in the trunk of our car an extra gallon of water and coolant, just in case we run into some overheating problems. We also carry with us flares in the event we need to warn other drivers, and a small tool kit in case someone stops to help who knows what he or she is doing. In our glove compartment is a flashlight with extra batteries and a first-aid kit. We think it is also wise to have on board some "emergency provisions" just in case we run into automotive trouble that takes time. Thus, we have enough food and drinking water to survive the duration, and have a blanket or sleeping bag to keep us warm. Nights can be cool, even in summer.

We don't mean to be overly dramatic about automotive concerns, but one cannot be too careful in this regard. We think it is far better to be prepared for the worst than to be unprepared and suffer the consequences.

FISHING AND HUNTING INFORMATION

Fishing and hunting regulations vary in each of the states we will visit. For more information about fishing and hunting seasons, licenses, regulations, and restrictions, please contact the appropriate agency in each state. These are:

In Arizona
Game and Fish Commission
2222 West Greenway Road
Phoenix, Arizona 85023, U.S.A.

In Colorado
Colorado Division of Wildlife
6060 Broadway Drive
Denver, Colorado 80216, U.S.A.

In New Mexico
Department of Game and Fish
Villagra Building
Santa Fe, New Mexico 87503,
   U.S.A.

In Utah
Division of Wildlife Resources
1596 West North Temple Street
Salt Lake City, Utah 84116,
   U.S.A.

MAPS AND GUIDEBOOKS

Good travelers use good maps. Most U.S. citizens, however, simply grab an "oil company" map which provides little but routes, towns, distances, and the locations of the oil company's gas stations. If you look at the fine print at the edge of these maps, you will discover that most "oil company" maps are made by two companies: Gousha or Rand McNally. These companies are certainly accomplished distributors, it seems.

Veteran world travelers are rightly appalled that most U.S. citizens do not avail themselves of more informative travel materials before, during, and even after a trip. Fine maps are especially useful when the traveler is in mountainous country, as we will be. Sophisticated travelers appreciate maps that depict topography, vegetation, railroads, political boundaries, schools, airports, mines, oil fields, streams, and the like (but not gas stations).

The best maps for travel in the United States are the 1:250,000-scale topographic quadrangles of the U.S. Geological Survey; this scale is appropriate for automotive travel. The maps are available from numerous map stores in larger cities (refer to the "Yellow Pages" of the telephone directory for information) and from the U.S. Department of the Interior, Geological Survey, Denver Federal Center, Denver, Colorado 80225, U.S.A. Also, at the state welcome centers on the interstate and at other locations (such as tourist information centers in towns, which often are Chamber of Commerce offices), one can obtain official state highway maps. This is true for the states we will visit: Colorado, New Mexico, Utah, and Arizona. Utah has an especially fine state map.

In addition to good maps for travel, take along an authoritative, single-volume encyclopedia; it can answer thousands of queries that will emerge during any highway or byway trip. Though it is heavy and oversized, our favorite by far is the unabridged, 3,000-page *New Columbia Encyclopedia*. It is worth every nickel you spend on it, even if you have to pay full retail price, and we never leave home on a trip such as *Beyond the Great Divide* without it.

Remember, too, that guidebooks are a special consideration and one should be careful about which ones to buy. Many of the best are mentioned in the "Suggested Readings" section of this field guide. Many so-called guidebooks, unfortunately, have little substance (despite their claims to the contrary) or are little more than lodging and restaurant directories subject to influence from advertising revenues (thus, they are not always reliable and miss many a good place to sleep and eat). It is hoped that you have a perspective beyond bed and belly!

The most accomplished travelers always obtain at least one authoritative, overall guidebook plus three or more specialized or topical guidebooks that fit their particular interests, such as those devoted solely to wildflowers, birds, trees and shrubs, geology, history and historic structures and places, fishing, rafting, or covered bridges. On one of our more recent outings with the New Mexico Geographical Society, for example, we came prepared with two dozen guidebooks and still had to pick up a couple more in transit to cover all the interests of our paying passengers! But the old reliable was still the *New Columbia Encyclopedia*.

NATIONAL PARK SERVICE PASSPORTS

The traveler should review the three types of passports currently available to determine if savings can be had at any federal entrance fee area in the United States, including the national parks. According to government legalese, a fee area is any designated entrance fee area of the National Park System that is administered by the National Park Service or the Department of the Interior. If you are eligible for a passport, then you can claim or purchase it, which-ever the case may be, at either the *first* national park you visit that has an entrance fee gate or at the visitor center of that national park (in the event the entrance fee gate is closed on arrival, for you still have tc pay on your way out of the park).

Herewith the three types of passports:

Golden Access Passport

This passport is available, at no charge, to anyone who is handi-capped. The government defines "handicapped" as anyone who is medically determined to be blind or permanently disabled for purposes of receiving benefits under federal law.

This passport provides free lifetime admission to any federal entrance fee area, including the national parks. The passport also admits the vehicle, the driver of the vehicle, and all other occu-pants in the vehicle without a fee. Thus, if the holder of the passport is not driving the vehicle, he or she should simply let the driver of the vehicle present the passport at the entrance fee gate in order to gain free admission for everyone.

Every so often a ranger will be unfamiliar with these rules and question you about them, but the rules described above come directly from the National Park Service, so don't let a young ranger tell you otherwise.

Golden Age Passport

This passport is available, at no charge, to any U.S. citizen who is 62 years old or older. It provides free lifetime admission to any federal entrance fee area, including the national parks. The pass-port also admits the vehicle, the driver of the vehicle, and all other occupants in the vehicle without a fee. Thus, if the holder of the passport is not driving the vehicle, she or he should simply let the driver of the vehicle present the passport at the entrance fee gate in order to gain free admission for everyone. Don't let an unknowing ranger tell you otherwise, for the rules described above come directly from the National Park Service.

In addition, this passport entitles the holder to a 50 percent discount on camping within the national parks. Many holders of the Golden Age Passport are unfamiliar with this perk.

Golden Eagle Passport

Currently, most of the major national parks and many of the smaller ones charge an admission of $5.00 per visit (good up to seven days with your receipt). Thus, if one plans to make a total of six or more visits to any national park in a given calendar year, then it is wise to purchase this passport for a current fee of $25.00.

This passport is available to anyone—U.S. citizen, foreigner, undocumented alien, or visitor from Mars. It entitles the holder to free admission to any federal entrance fee area, including the national parks, during the time when the card is in force (to repeat: the passport is good for one calendar year). The passport also admits the vehicle, the driver of the vehicle, and all other occupants in the vehicle without a fee. Thus, if the holder of the passport is not driving the vehicle, he or she should simply let the driver of the vehicle present the passport at the entrance fee gate in order to gain free admission for everyone. Every so often a ranger is not as familiar with these provisions as she or he should be, but the rules described above come directly from the National Park Service, so don't let the ranger tell you otherwise.

Note: In addition to the Golden Eagle Passport, some national parks offer their own annual discount passport. For example, at the beautiful Shenandoah National Park (SNP) in Virginia, the park offers an annual passport that is good for SNP visitation only. For an annual fee of $15.00, one can visit SNP as many times during the year as one wants, at no further charge. But the passport is good only at SNP. Since the entrance fee at SNP is $5.00 per visit (good up to seven days with a receipt), the SNP passport makes sense for anyone who visits the park four or more times a year, but doesn't visit any other national park or federal entrance fee area.

If, however, one wishes to visit SNP *and* another national park or federal entrance fee area for a total of six or more times in a given year, then it makes sense to buy the Golden Eagle Passport described above, and not the SNP passport.

This same scenario may apply to many of the national parks we plan to visit on our route or on one or more of the sidetrips. Check with those national parks to determine the conditions of its passport program (and if it offers one), and then determine the most economical way to proceed.

WEATHER

Many people who are visiting the Southern Rocky Mountains or the Colorado Plateau for the first time assume incorrectly that all parts of our route—but especially those places in New Mexico, Arizona, and Utah—are warm and seasonable year round. This is not the case. Although one can expect a climate that suits most people, winters can be hard in terms of the amount of snow and cold, even in areas most people associate with the Southwest. So one must be careful about what clothing to bring, depending on the time of year one plans to visit.

The most sensible advice we can give is this: Each traveler should rely on layers of clothing at all times of the year, and to have at least one warm sweater, a windbreaker, and a jacket on hand, too. Such an approach will protect you from the cool evenings that are common even in summer, from the windy conditions that can put a chill on even the hardiest of women and men in fall and spring, and from the wide range of temperature variations that we experience on this tour because of the changing elevation. Remember that we begin our journey in Denver at 5,280 feet, head west into the Rocky Mountains which tower over 14,000 feet and where we spend a lot of time between 7,000 and 11,000 feet, and end up in Kingman, Arizona, at 3,336 feet. At all elevations, it is wise to use sun screen, even when temperatures are cool.

When you visit the region affects the temperatures and amounts and types of precipitation you will likely run into. Obviously, in winter one dresses warmly, so there is no point belaboring the obvious (although many skiers are enjoying the slopes in short sleeves on occasion). But whereas most travelers expect to experience snow in the higher elevations of Colorado year-round, few first-time visitors realize that snow can be heavy and temperatures very cold as late as March and April in all parts of our journey. Although most of you can rightfully expect to experience hot conditions in the canyonlands of Utah and the lower reaches of the Grand Canyon in the summer, most of you will be surprised to learn that summer temperatures in Taos and Santa Fe rarely exceed a comfortable 85 degrees Fahrenheit. Just because a town is located in Arizona or New Mexico does not mean that this is the desert. Far from it. Taos and Santa Fe and Durango are not Phoenix in any way, shape, or form, except for one thing: persistent low humidity. This is the dry West, so do not expect the high humidity of the East, South, or Middle West. Low humidity is one of the great joys of living in the Interior West and Southwest, even if it leads to dry skin and heavy expenditures for lip balm and moisturizing creams and lotions.

One last item that may be of help to you. In advance of your trip beyond the Great Divide, try to watch the Weather Channel on cable television. This is the most accurate way to follow weather patterns for the region we are to cover, and thus to estimate the kind of temperatures and amount and type of precipitation you might run into. Then, during your trip, most of the motels and other lodging establishments you will be staying at will offer cable television and the Weather Channel. We have always found it useful to make a nightly check of the local weather on this channel, so we are prepared for conditions on the following day. Newspapers are good sources of information, too.

△ Suggested Readings

The literature on the Southwest and Interior West is as rich and varied as the region itself, and one can, quite literally, spend a lifetime just catching up on all the books that have been published, not to mention the time it would take to keep up with the plethora of new material that is published each year, as if books are to be gobbled up like M&Ms.

Below is a compendium of those books that, we believe, offer the common reader and serious traveler a fine overview of the literature on the region, with special attention given, of course, to how these books relate to *Beyond the Great Divide*. You may recall that, in the field guide itself, we refer, on occasion, to over a dozen books (some of which are included below) that relate specifically to certain segments of the tour. Broad subject categories are provided (Art and Photography, Geology and Physiography, Guidebooks and Series, History and Culture, Literature, and Maps and Reference Works) to facilitate your personal search for information and knowledge.

ART AND PHOTOGRAPHY

Robert Adams, not to be confused with Ansel Adams (b. 1902; d. 1984), is a renowned photographer from Longmont, Colorado, who has specialized in the interpretation of landscape and of place. Two of his earliest works are of interest to us here, not only because they deal with Denver and the Front Range, but also because these books have earned a place in the history of documentary photography of the American West. The two books we refer to are *The New West: Landscapes Along the Colorado Front Range* (Colorado Associated University Presses, 1974) and *Denver: A Photographic Survey of the Metropolitan Area* (Colorado Associated University Presses, 1977, in association with the State Historical Society of Colorado).

We spoke, with great admiration, of the scientific surveys and expeditions in the nineteenth century, in which professional painters and photographers worked alongside professional journalists, scientists, and surveyors to provide a comprehensive interpretation of the West's landscapes, which (at the time) were foreign to most Americans in the East. Two of our favorite books that recount some of the photographic contributions to these surveys are *The Western Photographs of John K. Hillers: Myself in the Water,* by Don D. Fowler (Smithsonian Institution Press, 1989), and *American Frontiers: The Photographs of Timothy H. O'Sullivan, 1867–1874,* by Joel Snyder (Aperture, 1981).

A photographic essay that has received a lot of attention is *Route 66: The Highway and Its People,* by Quinta Scott and Susan Croce Kelly (University of Oklahoma Press, 1988). The pictures and text unfold the story of this great highway, which linked Chicago with Los Angeles through New Mexico and Arizona and which was so significant in the country's social change in the early twentieth century.

As we note in the field guide, many artists and photographers have been attracted to Taos and New Mexico. Perhaps the best known of that group today is Georgia O'Keeffe, the painter. For a retrospective of her life's work, consult *Georgia O'Keeffe: In the West,* edited by Doris Bry and Nicholas Callaway (Alfred A. Knopf, 1989, in association with Callaway Editions). Ninety-eight color plates are featured, in addition to an historical text on her life and career. This is the book that accompanied the traveling museum exhibition of O'Keeffe's work.

Many fine books deal with Indian arts and crafts, but we believe the first book one should buy is *Navajo Rugs: Past, Present, and Future,* by Gilbert S. Maxwell (Desert-Southwest of Palm Springs, California, 1963; revised edition, 1984, by Santa Fe Images). Now in its twenty-third printing, the book is the standard guide to contemporary Indian weaving and, thus, it is widely available in bookstores and museum shops throughout the Southwest. Six new chapters appear in the latest edition to update this art form, and they do not disturb Maxwell's original text. Numerous black-and-white and color photographs of Navajo rugs are included.

With respect to Pueblo pottery, two books we recommend are *Seven Families in Pueblo Pottery,* offered by the University of New Mexico's

Maxwell Museum of Anthropology (University of New Mexico Press, 1974), and *Santa Clara Pottery Today,* by Betty LeFree (University of New Mexico Press, 1975, for the School of American Research). *Seven Families,* now in its fourteenth printing, traces the developments in style and technique in the pottery produced by seven Pueblo families. The black-and-white and color photographs represent a nearly complete chronological sequence of the potter's art within each family. *Santa Clara,* now in its tenth printing, is a more extensive search into the evolution of Santa Clara pottery. The author has recorded and photographed each step in the making of contemporary Santa Clara pottery, from the clay pit to the market. The reader will have a firm grasp of what Pueblo pottery involves after reading these two fine books.

GEOLOGY AND PHYSIOGRAPHY

Most travelers to the West are impressed by its landforms and most want to know more about the region's geology, but in language that is clear and understandable. Most wayfarers in the Southern Rocky Mountains and the Colorado Plateau, therefore, find the Roadside Geology Series informative and a real asset to enlightened travel. These noteworthy publications about rocks and landforms are written in readily comprehensive language and without too much jargon, and the material is especially useful because it is organized by routes of travel within each state. For our region, consult *Roadside Geology of Arizona* (1983), *Roadside Geology of Colorado* (1980), *Roadside Geology of New Mexico* (1987), and *Roadside Geology of Utah* (1990). All four books are written by Halka Chronic and are published by Mountain Press Publishing in Missoula, Montana.

The classic references on regional geomorphology of the United States are Nevin M. Fenneman's two-volume set, *Physiography of Western United States* (McGraw-Hill, 1931) and *Physiography of Eastern United States* (McGraw-Hill, 1938). These books, long out-of-print, are sought by book collectors, and rightfully so! They are prized volumes that belong in every collection of Americana.

A valuable addition to the two volumes by Fenneman is *Regional Geomorphology of the United States,* by William D. Thornbury (John Wiley and Sons, 1965). This work incorporates more recent material and includes significant references on geomorphology that have appeared subsequent to Fenneman's books. Both Fenneman and Thornbury display a grasp of the English language that few scholars in physical geography can emulate today. This is another reason these books are so valuable; they read almost like good fiction and allow the reader to imagine what the landscapes actually look like.

GUIDEBOOKS AND SERIES

In addition to the Roadside Geology Series mentioned above, we have field-tested and proved the value of several other guidebooks and series.

New Mexico: A New Guide to the Colorful State, by Lance Chilton *et alia* (University of New Mexico Press, 1984), is well written, well illustrated, and includes simple but appropriately designed maps. Most American guidebooks are boring, uninspired, trivial, tedious, and distressfully commercial. This book is a remarkable exception to these bed-and-breakfast directories.

New Mexico Place Names: A Geographical Dictionary, edited by T. M. Pearce (University of New Mexico Press, 1965), is now in its eighth printing, and one can understand why. It is a superb reference work, one of the best we've seen in the genre. Also of use is *Arizona Place Names,* by William C. Barnes (University of Arizona Press, 1988), and *Utah Place Names,* by John W. Van Cott (University of Utah Press, 1990). We've yet to come across a similar volume for Colorado.

The *Rivers of America* series comprises, in hindsight, a mixed bag of wonderful and above-average books about some of the nation's important rivers. Among the best, however, is *The Colorado,* by Frank Waters (Rinehart and Company, 1946; reprinted by Ohio University Press, 1985). To get a taste of the language, herewith the first four lines of the book: "Most rivers are confined to the needs and histories of men. Like roads, they seem inconsequential without their travelers. The Colorado is an outlaw. It belongs only to the ancient, eternal earth." One wonders if

Waters agreed with the harnessing of the river by such feats as the Glen Canyon Dam. Also in the series and of interest for our region is *The Arkansas,* by Clyde Brion Davis, which is out of print.

The *Smithsonian Guide to Historic America* is a twelve-volume set that is organized by region (and apparently not in consultation with geographers). Two volumes pertain to our tour: Volume 8: *The Rocky Mountain States* (Colorado, Wyoming, Idaho, and Montana), text by Jerry Camarillo Dunn (Stewart, Tabori, and Chang, 1989), and Volume 10: *The Desert States* (New Mexico, Arizona, Nevada, and Utah), text by Michael S. Durham (Stewart, Tabori, and Chang, 1990). These volumes are well prepared, contain gorgeous color and black-and-white photographs, display a very accomplished book design, and are handy in almost every way. Had the series reflected more accurately the actual number of geographical and cultural regions in the United States, however, there would have been more than twelve volumes. And had there been more than twelve volumes, each individual volume could have been more comprehensive in its coverage of places, sites, events, and the like.

Tom Snyder's *Route Sixty-six Traveler's Guide* (St. Martin's, 1990) has received a lot of media attention, and it is a necessary complement to the Scott and Kelly book mentioned above in the "Art and Photography" section.

The States and the Nation series was published for the national Bicentennial of the American Revolution by W. W. Norton and the American Association for State and Local History, with financial support provided, in part, by the National Endowment for the Humanities. These are historical, not geographical, interpretations of the development of each state in the union, and most, if not all, of the volumes are quite accomplished. For our region, consult *Arizona: A History,* by Lawrence C. Powell (W. W. Norton, 1976; University of New Mexico Press, 1990), *Colorado: A History,* by Marshall Sprague (W. W. Norton, 1976), *New Mexico: A History,* by Marc Simmons (W. W. Norton, 1977), and *Utah: A History,* by Charles S. Peterson (W. W. Norton, 1977).

The reader might be surprised by the following entry: *Wildflowers of Zion National Park,* by Stanley L. Welsh (Zion Natural History Association, 1990). We do not visit Zion on our regular route, nor do we visit Zion on a side trip (though every U.S. citizen should, at some point in his or her life, spend some time in this magnificent national park); still, this compact, handsome, and informative field guide is a very handy reference throughout our region. Approximately 900 different kinds of plants are known within Zion National Park, and many of them are present on our route. This book covers 120 of the most common flowers, shrubs, and trees, and the book's only flaw is that it fails to include a few more. The book is a gem, however, and we wish more "nature guides" were as well-written, user-friendly, and attractive as this book by Dr. Welsh.

Although no one wants to experience another Great Depression, or even a recession such as the one in the early 1990s, most of us believe that a few programs emerged (for a brief period) during the 1930s that might be worth bringing out of the attic, such as the Civilian Conservation Corps. One of the great projects of the 1930s was the Federal Writers Project of the Works Progress Administration, which included guides for every state in the union and for many major cities. They were the most comprehensive and the best tour guides ever written in the United States. Long ago the originals (i.e., the first editions) went out of print, and now even subsequent (out-of-print) hardcover printings garner a good price in the used book stores.

Thankfully, though, the WPA/FWP books have been reprinted in paperback, and many of them updated, with varying degrees of success. Veteran travelers find the guides as useful today as ever; in some ways, they are more significant now as we travel over highways and byways and observe the many changes in the landscape from yesteryears. If you cannot obtain copies readily, remember that most public libraries (at least those that haven't been closed or underfunded) have them for loan. For our region, consult *Arizona: The Grand Canyon State* (Hastings House, 1940; reprinted, 1989), *Colorado: A Guide to the Highest State* (Hastings House, 1941; reprinted, 1989), *New Mexico: A Guide to the Colorful State* (Hastings House, 1940; reprinted, 1989), and *Utah: A Guide to the State* (Hastings House, 1941; reprinted, 1989).

HISTORY AND CULTURE

The historical and archeological/anthropological literature on the region is immense, so please understand our predicament that we must be selective due to the lack of space. Still, the following books are worthy of any traveler's bookshelf, and no doubt they will provide immense pleasure when you return home and reminisce in the comfort of your own armchair.

Great Surveys of the American West, by Richard A. Bartlett (University of Oklahoma Press, 1962), is an account of the four "Great Surveys" of the West by the U.S. government from 1867 to 1879 that we refer to in Part I of this field guide. These expeditions of Ferdinand Vandeveer Hayden, Clarence King, John Wesley Powell, and George Montague Wheeler, you will recall, comprised a team of professional surveyors, scientists, photographers, painters, and journalists. This book is an exciting record of scientific exploration and a reminder to today's research institutions that this approach to the study of place makes even more sense today than in the good old days. This book is vicarious adventure at its finest!

The Spanish-American Homeland: Four Centuries in New Mexico's Río Arriba, by Alvar W. Carlson (Johns Hopkins University Press, 1990), is a book we refer to frequently in the field guide. It is a monumental contribution based upon meticulous archival research and decades of field observation by one of the outstanding geographers in the United States. Despite its scholarly inclinations, however, it is highly readable, appropriately illustrated with photographs, maps, and diagrams, and offers a unique insight into the evolution of this distinctive cultural hearth that was settled permanently by the Spanish in 1598, over two decades before the Pilgrims landed on Plymouth Rock in Massachusetts. It's amazing how the standard textbooks in U.S. history dismiss the contributions of the Spanish in the early development of our nation, especially in the West. The book appears as the sixth volume in George F. Thompson's award-winning series, "Creating the North American Landscape."

Mayordomo: Chronicle of an Acequia in Northern New Mexico, by Stanley Crawford (University of New Mexico Press, 1988), received the 1988 Western States Book Award for Creative Nonfiction. This is a memorable account of the life-giving water that an irrigation ditch brings to a community, and how the maintenance of that ditch binds an entire community together. Of equal value is *River of Traps: A Village Life,* by William deBuys and Alex Harris (University of New Mexico Press,

1990, in association with the Center for Documentary Studies at Duke University). This distinctive work is not only a tribute to the art of making books, but also an unusually moving portrait of three men—two Anglos (the authors) and Jacobo Romero (an old farmer whose family has long lived in the area)—and of the place that continually shaped their lives—a small, isolated mountain village in northern New Mexico. Readers of these books, plus Carlson's *magnum opus,* will gain a real insight into the traditions of this very special region in the United States. And readers are also encouraged to buy first editions of these books while they last, for all three are destined to become classics and to be valued by book collectors in the years to come.

American Indians of the Southwest, by Bertha P. Dutton (University of New Mexico Press, 1903; revised, 1975), is a comprehensive compendium of Indian culture and history, and it includes authoritative material on archeology, tribal affairs, arts and crafts, and culture. The book was written by a distinguished anthropologist of the American Southwest whose field-work spanned a half century. Copies of the 1903 edition are rare.

We hesitate to include the following entry, simply because it is so big, but it is a classic: Paul Horgan's *Great River: The Rio Grande in North American History,* which contains two volumes, *Indians and Spain* (Volume 1) and *Mexico and the United States* (Volume 2). Originally published in 1954 by Rinehart, a 2¼-inch-thick paperback edition was released by Texas Monthly Press in 1984. Anyone who is seriously interested in the Southwest must know something about the Rio Grande, for there is no greater life-blood to the region. Paul Horgan's work is, as the London *Times Literary Supplement* says, "one of the most fascinating books in recent American historiography," but you will need a week's vacation on a beach in Mexico to read through its 1,138 printed pages, which isn't such a bad idea.

We would also like to mention again two other classics: *The Exploration of the Colorado River and Its Canyons* (1875 report; first published in 1895; reissued, unabridged, by Dover Publications in 1961) and *Report of the Lands of the Arid Region of the United States* (1879 report; reissued, unabridged, by Harvard Common Press in 1983), written by the dauntless, one-armed explorer, John Wesley Powell. Powell's account of the Colorado River expedition is one of the greatest adventure stories ever written. And for those who still yearn for an honest environmental approach for how to develop and not develop the arid Southwest, spend some time with Powell's *Report,* which politicians to this day still avoid because it makes so much sense.

Last, but not least, we recommend *Continuity and Continuity: The History, Architecture, and Cultural Landscape of La Tierra Amarilla,* by Chris Wilson and David Kammer (New Mexico Historic Preservation Division, 1989). This book is a valuable documentation of a precious cultural relict area in New Mexico's Río Arriba.

LITERATURE

Although one cannot deny the popularity of the Westerns by Louis L'Amour or the suspense thrillers of Tony Hillerman, our intent here is a little more serious, so that by literature we lean heavily toward "creative nonfiction" in spirit.

Edward Abbey wrote *Desert Solitaire* and it launched his esteemed literary career. Originally published by McGraw-Hill in 1968, a trade paperback was issued by Ballantine in 1971 and it remains a hot seller for Ballantine as a classic in American nature writing. In 1988, a year before Abbey's death, the University of Arizona Press reissued a hardcover edition that contains a new preface and handsome illustrations. The book is "must reading" for anyone who has an interest in the conservation movement in the United States, in nature writing, or in the canyonlands of Utah. This is an angry book, not a romantic treatise about how nice birds look.

Willa Cather (b. 1873; d. 1947), a Pulitzer Prize winner and one of the greatest writers the United States produced in the first half of the twentieth century, wrote twelve novels and a collection of short stories, many of which are considered classics in American fiction. We believe that, of all her books, her masterpiece is *Death Comes for the Archbishop* (Alfred A. Knopf, 1927; Random House, 1971), which, fortunately for the tour, is a book on colonial New Mexico and a great regional novel.

Leslie Marmon Silko is a celebrated writer who was raised on the Laguna Pueblo reservation in New Mexico west of Albuquerque. From

1981 to 1986 she received a MacArthur Foundation Fellowship (better known as the genius grant), at which time she began writing a long novel about the Indians of the Southwest. This novel, *Almanac of the Dead,* was published in 1991 by Simon and Schuster, and from all accounts it is an important book. It is also long. Silko is also the author of *Laguna Woman: Poems by Leslie Marmon Silko* (Greenfield Review Press, 1974) and *Ceremony* (Viking, 1977; Signet, 1978), but we recommend that you read *Storyteller* (Seaver Books/Grove Press, 1981). Storytelling is the means by which Indian tribes and nations communicated from one generation to the next their feats, legends, and religious beliefs. The stories often had a mystical quality. In this book, Silko re-creates the ancient stories, in prose and poetry, and integrates them with the realities of her own experience on the reservation. It is a most unusual and important book.

We also encourage our readers to purchase a copy of Reg Saner's book, *The Four-Cornered Falcon: Essays on the Interior West and the Natural Scene,* which will be available for sale from the Johns Hopkins University Press in the spring of 1993. This is the fourteenth volume in the "Creating the North American Landscape" series, and its subject is the relationship between human beings and their natural world, especially in the mountains, canyons, deserts, and forests of Colorado, New Mexico, Utah, and Arizona. Saner, who lives in Boulder, Colorado, is an internationally recognized writer and poet, and the book will surely become an American land classic.

MAPS AND REFERENCE WORKS

We remind all travelers to obtain from the United States Geological Survey in Denver (for the address, see "Hints to the Traveler"), or from a good map store the *U.S.G.S. Topographical Maps.* In addition to elevations, topographic sheets locate transportation routes, schools, forested areas, political boundaries, mines, and the names of streams, towns, and the like. Travelers in Europe have long used this type of map. Astute U.S. citizens, rightfully frustrated with "oil company" maps, are delighted to obtain these for travel—particularly in such rugged lands as those found in the Interior West and Southwest. Most useful for automobile travel are those maps scaled 1:250,000.

We also remind all travelers to bring along the *New Columbia Encyclopedia* (unabridged version), if at all possible. On the tour's route you will have hundreds of questions about the land, the people, events, and other matters that can best be answered by referring to this treasure trove of information. Your tour will be enhanced and enriched if you don't leave home without it. A new edition is available in late 1993.

Finally, we wish to pay tribute to two of the greatest geographies of America ever written. They appeared over a half-century ago, before the advent of the Nuclear Age, in a period of time and culture when our schools, colleges, and universities were far different than they are today, in spirit and function and size. Then—and we are not waxing sentimental about the good old days—teachers, students, and administrators alike shared a common purpose that was best reflected in the old biblical credo of learning: "With all thy getting, get understanding." Today, we are complacent about this directive and the wisdom it implies (there's no money in it), and we allow our schools, colleges, and universities to became more market-oriented, more product-driven, more corporate, more factory-like every year. Thus, it is significant that we mention these two great geographical works, for they stand, taller than ever, as achievements that were possible and encouraged in that earlier, freer age, and as monuments to human insight, to the beauty of informed scholarship, to the love of learning, and to the cultivation of western civilization through books and the development of an educated citizenry. It was, after all, an educated citizenry that Thomas Jefferson believed was and is the key to maintaining a free, democratic society.

The first of these books was written by the late Henri Baulig, a French professor at the University of Strasbourg. It appeared in the renowned series, *Géographie Universelle,* and it is entitled, simply and convincingly, *États-Unis.* It was published in 1936 by Librairie Armond Colin under the direction of P. Vidal de La Blache and L. Gallois. This book is so valuable because it offers a foreigner's straightforward observation of the United States. It is, in that regard, comparable to Alexis de Tocqueville's *Democracy in America* (1835), which was so influential in its day; or even to *The Economist* of today, that great weekly magazine based in London that provides us with a regular opportunity to read how foreigners view the United States. The book contains numerous diagrams and photographs, and its maps, so artfully conceived and drawn, remain an inspiration to those of us who are mystified by the current obsession with computer-generated cartographics, which so often deny the entry of art and common sense into the making of maps. The book was written in French.

The second book is entitled, simply and convincingly, *North America.* Its author is the late J. Russell Smith, an American professor of geography at Columbia University in New York City when the Ivy League school still had a department of geography. The book was published in 1925 by Harcourt, Brace. It was written in English, American.

We encourage all readers of *Beyond the Great Divide* to locate these two great books, long out of print, and to read them at your leisure until your heart is content. You will not be disappointed. They will assist any serious traveler in his or her attempt to read the American landscape, and this can involve a lifetime of travel and learning.

△ Index